THE ULTIMATE WRESTLING QUIZ BOOK

ONE THOUSAND QUESTIONS ON THE HISTORY OF PRO-WRESTLING

Benjamin A. Richardson

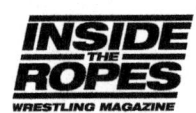

INSIDE THE ROPES
WRESTLING MAGAZINE

www.insidetheropesmagazine.com

Copyright © Benjamin A. Richardson, 2021

Published by Titan Insider Press
contact@titaninsiderpress.com

All rights reserved. No part of this publication may be reproduced, stored in a retrieval system, or transmitted in any form by any process — electronic, mechanical, photocopying, recording, or otherwise — without the prior written permission of the copyright holders and Titan Insider Press. The scanning, uploading, and distribution of this book via the Internet or via any other means without the permission of the publisher is illegal and punishable by law. Please purchase only authorized electronic editions, and do not participate in or encourage electronic piracy of copyrighted materials.
Your support of the authors' rights is appreciated.

Designed and typeset by STK Design
Cover design by STK Design
Cover images: John Barrett (Hulk Hogan, Steve Austin), Scott Lesh (Britt Baker), ITR Archive (Mitsuharu Misawa & Toshiaki Kawada, Bret Hart), Bill Otton (John Cena)
Back cover images: Scott Lesh (Kenny Omega), John Barrett (Ric Flair), ITR Archive (Shinya Hashimoto, The Iron Sheik & Hulk Hogan, Booker T)

First edition: 2021.

Printed and bound in the United Kingdom

www.insidetheropesmagazine.com

CONTENTS

CHAPTER ONE	THE PIONEERS	5
CHAPTER TWO	THE TERRITORIES	13
CHAPTER THREE	THE GOLDEN ERA	29
CHAPTER FOUR	A NEW GENERATION	45
CHAPTER FIVE	ATTITUDE	63
CHAPTER SIX	THE MONOPOLY	79
CHAPTER SEVEN	THE PG ERA	97
CHAPTER EIGHT	THE NETWORK	111
CHAPTER NINE	BEING ELITE	127
CHAPTER TEN	PURORESU	143
CHAPTER ELEVEN	LETHAL LOTTERY	159
ANSWERS		167
PHOTO CREDITS		230

CHAPTER ONE

THE PIONEERS

(Answers: P. 167)

1. What was the nickname shared by Wisconsin wrestlers Evan Lewis and his namesake Ed Lewis?

2. Which American President was known as one of the most fearsome wrestlers of the 1830s?

3. Ed Lewis wrestled over 6,000 matches in his wrestling career. How many did he lose?

    a) 0 **b)** 17 **c)** 32 **d)** 14

4. Which Iowa-born catch wrestler would make a show of his unnaturally strong neck by surviving a hangman's noose, and then whistling *Yankee Doodle*?

5. Wrestlers Karl Gotch and Simon Gotch both took their ring names from which wrestler, described by *Pro Wrestling Illustrated* as the 'best North American wrestler of the 20th century'?

6. What sporting event, first held in Braemar, Scotland in 1837, helped popularise Cumberland wrestling within Great Britain?

7. Which common professional wrestling move is George Hackenschmidt believed to have invented?

THE ULTIMATE WRESTLING QUIZ BOOK

8. On 10 March 1870, James McLaughlin defeated Barney Smith to win professional wrestling's first what?

9. True or false? McLaughlin served as a Colonel in the United States Civil War.

10. For which British monarch did catch-as-catch-can star Edwin Bibby perform in London in the 1870s?

11. William Miller vs. Clarence Whistler on 26 September 1885 was the first professional wrestling match held in which country?

12. Whistler died of internal bleeding shortly after the above contest, after eating what in celebration?

13. The very first wrestling trading cards were packaged with what Allen & Ginter Company product in 1887?

14. Yusuf 'the Terrible Turk' Ismail successfully challenged Evan Lewis for which championship in 1898?

15. Carl Abs, one of the 19th century's most celebrated German professional wrestlers, was nicknamed after what type of hard-wearing tree?

WM. MULDOON.
ALLEN & GINTER'S

THE PIONEERS

16. In 1903, Scottish strongman Donald Dinnie, known as 'the 19th Century's Strongest Athlete', endorsed which Scottish soft drink?

17. A national hero in his homeland, Jim Londos once drew a crowd of 100,000 fans when he returned to wrestle in which European country?

18. Because of their ability to stretch and bend an opponent's limbs, catch wrestlers were also known by what term?

19. How did Cora Livingston make professional wrestling history in October 1910?

20. Joe Stecher and Ed Lewis' rematch in Omaha, NE on 5 July 1915 ended in a draw after approximately how long?

   a) 2 hours b) 3 hours c) 4 hours d) 5 hours

21. What name, taken from a fictional Polish knight, was given to Jan Stanislaw Cyganiewicz and later adopted by a two-time AWA champion?

22. Promoters Toots Mondt, Ed Lewis and Billy Sandow were collectively known as what?

23. True or false? Jackie Chan based much of his training routine on that of Indian strongman and undefeated wrestling champion The Great Gama.

24. The first wrestler in the United States to wear a mask was known as what?

   a) The Masked Marvel   b) The Masked Wrestler
   c) The Masked Assassin d) The Masked Man

THE ULTIMATE WRESTLING QUIZ BOOK

25. Which 1925 world championship match infamously ended with a legitimate double-cross in favour of the challenger?

26. What was the nickname of New York-born Greco-Roman wrestler William Muldoon?

27. What was Maurice Tillet, born 23 October 1903 in the Ural Mountains, Russia, better known as throughout his career?

28. What family name is associated with the New York booker Jess, whose son and grandson both became major promoters within the business?

29. True or false? The World Heavyweight Wrestling Championship was the first heavyweight professional wrestling championship in the United States.

30. What style of wrestling, later the name of a major wrestling pay-per-view, became massively popular in Britain during the 1930s?

31. 'Mexican Wrestling Enterprise' is the English translation of which *lucha libre* promotion, founded in 1933?

THE PIONEERS

32. What was the signature move of wrestler Danno O'Mahony, after which a promotion in his native Ireland was named?

33. Which professional wrestling move did Jim Londos introduce in June 1931, amidst controversy that it was a form of choke?

34. How old was Lou Thesz when he made his professional wrestling debut in 1932?

35. What sort of wrestling match took place for the first time on 25 June 1937?

36. Which wrestling hold did Ed Lewis gain a fearsome reputation for, after honing it daily on a wooden mannequin?

37. Armenian World Heavyweight Champion Arteen Ekizian was better known by what ring name, derived from Middle Eastern folk tale *One Thousand and One Nights*?

38. P.T. Barnum's Great Roman Hippodrome is considered the spiritual predecessor of which venue?

39. Italian-American wrestler Angelo Savoldi was allegedly friends with which best-selling American crooner during his childhood growing up in Hoboken, NJ?

40. What was the nickname of prominent Boston promoter Paul Bowser, latterly shared by a popular wrestling manager?

41. One time catch-as-catch-can World Heavyweight Champion Earl Craddock was the first wrestler to bill himself as what, a claim later made by Dean Malenko?

THE ULTIMATE WRESTLING QUIZ BOOK

42. True or false? Ed Lewis came out of wrestling retirement in 1942 despite being legally blind.

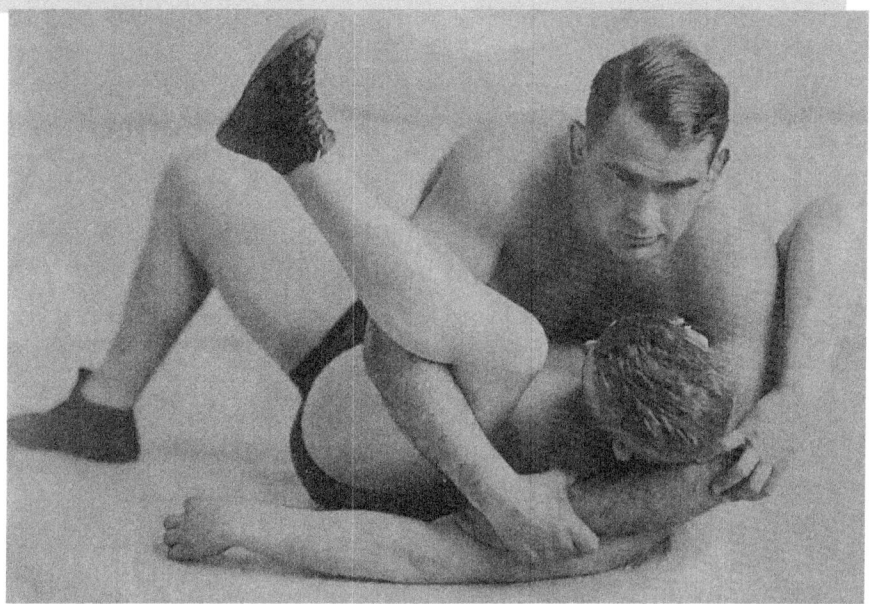

43. Which ceremonial English county is believed to be the birthplace of catch-as-catch-can wrestling?

    a) Lancashire   **b)** Cumbria
    c) North Yorkshire   **d)** Norfolk

44. In which country were wrestlers Georg Lurich, George Hackenschmidt and Aleksander Aberg all born?

45. The 'Nebraska Tiger Man' John Pesek was inducted into the *Wrestling Observer Newsletter* Hall of Fame in 1996. In which other sport's Hall of Fame is he also recognised?

46. At which esteemed military academy did three-time American Heavyweight Champion Tom Jenkins teach between 1905 and 1942?

THE PIONEERS

47. In 1947, Admiral-Lord Mountevans wrote up a set of unified rules in an attempt to formalise professional wrestling in the UK - and counter what claim against the sport?

48. Elgar's *Pomp and Circumstance March*, later adopted by Randy Savage, became wrestling's first theme music when which wrestler began using it as part of their entrance routine?

49. What was the name of the loose confederation of wrestling promotions formed in 1948?

50. True or false? Fred Kohler's *Wrestling from Marigold* became the first regular wrestling show on television when it launched on the DuMont Network in 1949.

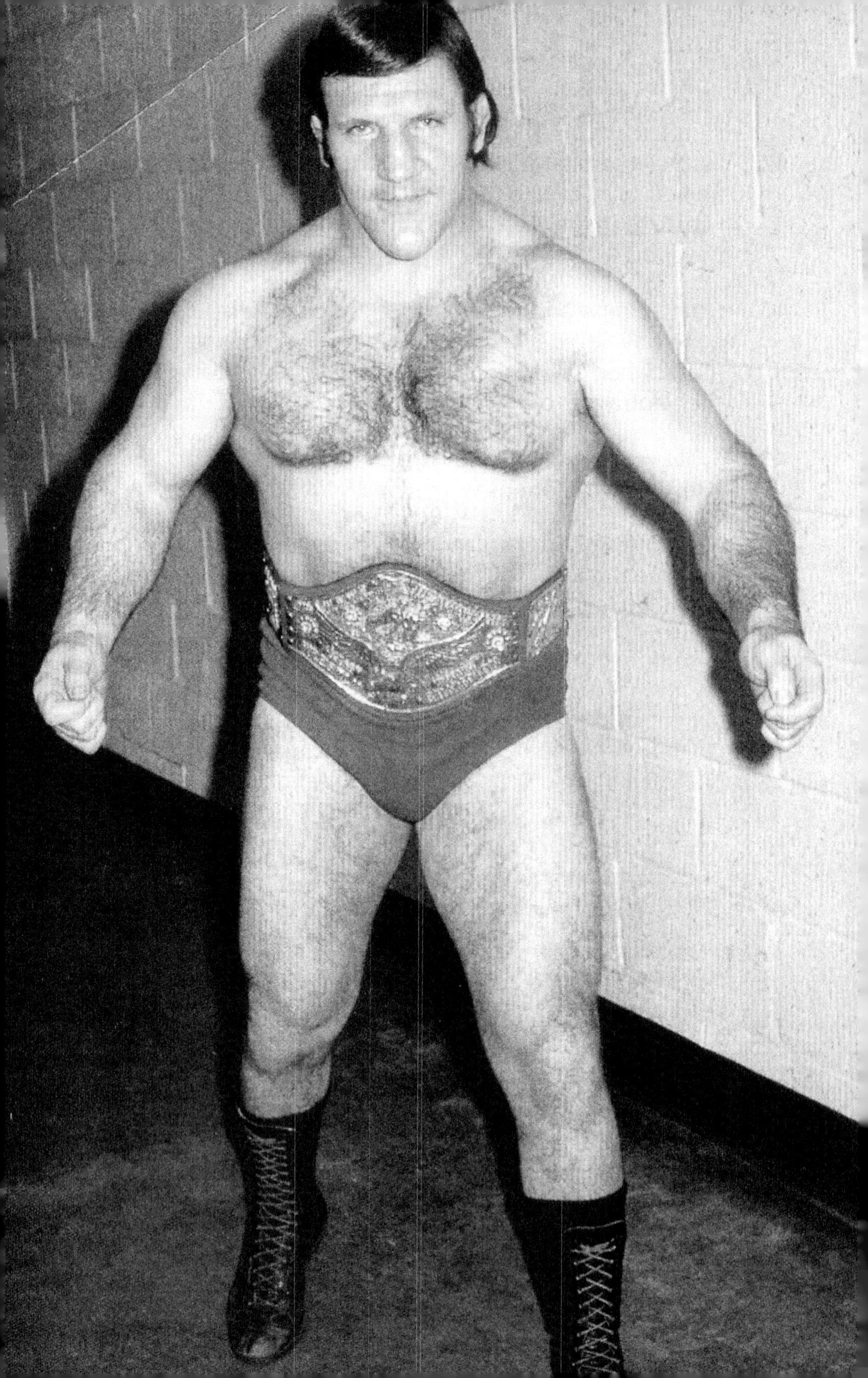

CHAPTER TWO

THE TERRITORIES

(Answers: P. 171)

1. In January 1952, the company that would one day become WWE ran its first show. What was its name?

2. Who became the first NWA World Heavyweight Champion upon the organisation's inception on 14 July 1948?

3. Which future NWA Hall of Famer wrestled their first known match on 29 March 1948 under the guise of 'Houston Harris, the Black Panther'?

4. In which city was Fritz von Erich's World Class Championship Wrestling based?

5. The American Wrestling Association (AWA) was founded in 1960 by Wally Karbo and which Minneapolis amateur and professional wrestler?

6. What did Stu Hart's Calgary-based Klondike Wrestling change its name to in 1967?

7. Which San Francisco Bay Area venue was the home of Roy Shire's Big Time Wrestling?

8. Which North Carolina wrestling promotion, established 1931, went by the names 'All Star Wrestling', 'Championship Wrestling', and 'East Coast Wrestling', amongst others?

THE ULTIMATE WRESTLING QUIZ BOOK

9. True or false? Despite winning more recognised wrestling championships than any wrestler in history, Jerry Lawler never held a belt in WWF/WWE.

10. Which country did Karl Gotch represent in both freestyle and Greco-Roman wrestling at the 1948 London Olympics?

11. What was the nickname of Paul George, the 'father of the NWA'?

12. How many days did Bruno Sammartino's record-setting first reign as WWWF World Heavyweight Champion last?

a) 1,262 **b)** 2,803 **c)** 3,450 **d)** 4,040

THE TERRITORIES

13. What was the name of the weekly television programme presented by Sam Muchnick's St. Louis Wrestling Club?

14. Which wrestling villain was renowned for his devastating 'Blonde Bomber' knee drop?

15. Which 13-time world champion was the first professional wrestler to adopt the moniker 'Nature Boy'?

16. Across how many reigns did Lou Thesz hold the NWA World Heavyweight Championship to set a record 3,749 days with the belt?

17. What was the combined weight of pro wrestling attractions the McGuire twins, listed in the *Guinness Book of World Records* as the 'world's heaviest twins'?

    a) 997lbs **b)** 1,112lbs **c)** 1,356lbs **d)** 1,468lbs

18. True or false? Terrible Ted, a wrestling bear that toured North American promotions in the '50s, '60s and '70s, once spent time in a jail in Lowndes County, GA.

19. Name the wrestler: born Édouard Ignacz Weiczorkiewicz on 17 July 1926, he regularly wowed audiences with a range of athletic moves such as back flips and somersaults.

20. 50th State Big Time Wrestling, founded in 1936 by Al Karasick, was based in which US state?

21. Which Oklahoma-born wrestler was known for his ability to crush an apple with one hand?

THE ULTIMATE WRESTLING QUIZ BOOK

22. What nickname links professional wrestlers Jerry Blackwell, Steve Casey, and Reginald Lisowski?

23. Which masked grappler is shown in the photo below?

24. What match, held 30 June 1961 in Comiskey Park, set the all-time NWA attendance record of 38,000?

25. True or false? Bruno Sammartino's 1964 WWWF World Heavyweight Championship defence against Waldo von Erich at Madison Square Garden ended in a draw because of an 11pm curfew on events in New York.

26. Which Canadian heel (who later trained Triple H, Perry Saturn, and Big John Studd, amongst others) claimed in the '60s to be wrestling's only vegetarian?

THE TERRITORIES

27. What surname links wrestlers Angelo, Randy, and Lanny?

28. True or false? Terry Funk made his professional wrestling debut in the same year future WWE star The Undertaker was born.

29. Name the wrestler, pictured below, who held the NWA World Women's Championship between 1937 and 1954?

30. What is the name of the non-profit fraternal organisation, established 1965, for active and retired wrestlers?

THE ULTIMATE WRESTLING QUIZ BOOK

31. Which eight-time NWA World Heavyweight Champion and member of wrestling's five most prestigious Halls of Fame got his break in the business as the driver for the gargantuan Happy Humphrey?

32. What weapon of choice was hardcore wrestling trailblazer Abdullah the Butcher known to rake across his opponents' faces?

33. What controversial flag did the Fabulous Freebirds often come to ring adorned, draped, or painted with?

34. Big Time Wrestling promoter Ed 'The Sheik' Farhat was the uncle of which ECW original?

35. Across a near five-decade wrestling career, *luchador* El Santo established himself as one of the greatest icons of not just Mexican wrestling, but Mexican society in general. What does 'El Santo' mean in English?

36. True or false? In 1973, future WWF commentator Gorilla Monsoon helped establish Carlos Colon's World Wrestling Council in Puerto Rico.

THE TERRITORIES

37. The third iteration of the NWA World Heavyweight Championship belt was used between 1974 and 1986, and revived in 1994 following the organisation's split from WCW. How many pounds of gold was it said to weigh?

38. Australian wrestlers Al Costello and Roy Heffernan were collectively known as what?

39. Dick Beyer was better known under what alias?

40. In 1987, future US President George Bush sent a telegram lauding the lifetime achievements of which veteran Houston promoter during a retirement show in his honour?

41. Who became 'Superstar' Billy Graham's manager when he joined WWWF in October 1975?

42. What in-ring 'feat' did Stan Hansen, Hulk Hogan, Kamala, and Harley Race all accomplish before it allegedly occurred for the first time in 1987?

43. Ric Flair's signature shout of 'Wooo!' was inspired by which 1957 pop song (after which a WWE pay-per-view was later named)?

44. What was the real name of World of Sport's original Kendo Nagasaki, a samurai with supposedly mystical healing powers?

45. Which of the following was *not* a legitimate member of the Von Erich family?

   a) Kevin b) Kerry c) Lance d) Mike

THE ULTIMATE WRESTLING QUIZ BOOK

46. True or false? The German Suplex is named in honour of Prussian villain Baron Von Raschke.

47. Action films *'Mystery in Bermuda'*, *'Black Power'*, and *'Enigma of Death'* all starred which legendary *luchador*?

48. True or false? Neither Chief Jay Strongbow nor Wahoo McDaniel were legitimate Native Americans.

49. What surname links The Fabulous Moolah and one of her protégées, Bette Boucher?

50. In which South American city did WWWF claim Pat Patterson won a tournament to become the company's first Intercontinental Champion?

51. True or false? Dick the Bruiser was banned for life from wrestling in New York after inciting a riot at Madison Square Garden in November 1957.

52. In what year did WWF withdraw from the National Wrestling Alliance for the second and final time?

53. Which wrestler portrayed Swedish grappler and B-movie star Tor Johnson in Tim Burton's 1994 film *Ed Wood*?

THE TERRITORIES

54. What surname linked storyline brothers Jimmy, Jerry, and Johnny during their lengthy WWWF run?

55. Which wrestler, known as 'The Universal Heartthrob', became the first NWA National Heavyweight Champion on 12 January 1980?

56. True or false? Ole Anderson is the brother of Arn Anderson.

57. Name the wrestler: nicknamed 'Bullet', he was a star of the Georgia territory for almost 30 years, and his four sons all followed him into the industry.

58. For what feat of strength was Austrian powerhouse Otto Wanz listed in the *Guinness Book of World Records*?

59. With which second-generation wrestler did Jim Brunzell form the High Flyers tag team in AWA?

60. True or false? Bruiser Brody also worked under the aliases Apache Jack and The Masked Mauler.

61. 'Pencil neck geek' was the favoured insult of which wrestler and manager, who even released a CD named for his catchphrase?

62. In 1996, Tracy Smothers began working for WWF under the moniker 'Freddie Joe Floyd'. After which brothers, stalwarts of the NWA territories, was he named?

THE ULTIMATE WRESTLING QUIZ BOOK

63. True or false? 'Exotic' Adrian Street, known for his flamboyant and sexually ambiguous persona, worked in a Welsh coal mine at the age of 15.

64. Which WWWF star was Vince McMahon such a big fan of that he bleached his hair to resemble him?

65. Name the wrestling announcer: born Francis Jonard Labiak, he provided the voice of promotions GCW, CCW, and WCW, amongst others.

66. From what animal, also known as a binturong, did wrestler Edward M. Wright take his nickname?

67. Which WWWF star and multiple Hall of Famer appeared in an episode of sitcom *That '70s Show*?

68. Which Irish playwright, best known for existential drama *Waiting for Godot*, occasionally drove a young Andre the Giant to school in his native France?

69. The lariat was the hard-hitting finishing move - and nickname - of which Texan wrestler?

70. What New York City law was lifted to allow Mil Máscaras to compete at Madison Square Garden on 18 December 1972?

71. Which usually-masked wrestler was Máscaras' opponent on this show, wrestling with his face exposed?

THE TERRITORIES

72. True or false? During his 15 May 1971 WWWF Heavyweight Championship match with Pedro Morales, Blackjack Mulligan was attacked by a fan wielding a gun.

73. What was the name of the British wrestling cartel operated by Max Crabtree during the sport's mid-'70s boom?

74. Which wrestler and American football player portrayed Mongo in Mel Brooks' 1974 comedy *Blazing Saddles*?

75. What WWF first did Pedro Morales (pictured) accomplish on 8 December 1980?

76. David Letterman's talk show ensemble, 'The World's Most Dangerous Band', was named in honour of which fellow Indianan, dubbed 'The World's Most Dangerous Wrestler'?

77. To what name did Bill Watts rebrand Leroy McGuirk's Tri-State Wrestling territory after purchasing it in 1979?

78. To which New York stadium did 36,295 fans flock to witness Bruno Sammartino exact revenge over Larry Zbyszko in a steel cage on 9 August 1980?

79. Which British super heavyweights headlined a card at Wembley Arena in front of 10,000 fans on 18 June 1981?

80. 'The Gateway to the Best' was the slogan of which wrestling promotion?

81. Heart of America Sports Attractions, founded by former NWA Champion Orville Brown in 1948, operated out of which Missouri city?

82. In which city did Roddy Piper refuse to work during his early WWF years, out of loyalty for promoter Don Owen?

83. How many of Stu and Helen Hart's eight sons followed their father into wrestling?

84. In 1979, Vince McMahon's WWWF rebranded as WWF. What did the 'W' discarded from the earlier acronym stand for?

85. In December 1981, which wrestler became the subject of *Sports Illustrated*'s longest ever profile on a single athlete?

THE TERRITORIES

86. What 'hometown' was shared by The Moondogs, The Executioners, and Missing Link?

87. True or false? British wrestling giant Big Daddy's birth name was Shirley.

88. On 7 September 1982, Jack Veneno defeated Ric Flair for the NWA World Heavyweight Championship, a victory that was never acknowledged by the governing body. In which Caribbean country did it take place?

89. Which star of Britain's World of Sport wrote a controversial warts-and-all autobiography called '*You Grunt, I'll Groan*' in 1985?

90. Which Memphis wrestler allegedly pulled a gun on Randy Savage prior to their real-life parking lot brawl in 1982?

THE ULTIMATE WRESTLING QUIZ BOOK

91. According to Hulk Hogan, he was fired from the WWF by Vince McMahon Sr. for starring in which 1982 Hollywood film?

92. The Junkyard Dog came to the ring to which Queen hit during his bounteous years in Mid-South Wrestling?

93. Which masked cruiserweight made headlines by capturing both NWA and WWF's junior heavyweight championships on consecutive nights in May 1982?

94. True or false? Wayne 'Honky Tonk Man' Ferris was part of the Midnight Express in 1983.

95. What was the name of the supercard regularly held at Texas Stadium in Irving, TX, between 1961 and 1988?

96. Who won the NWA World Heavyweight Championship in February 1982 under a mask as 'The Midnight Rider'?

97. Who infamously slammed a steel cage door onto Kerry von Erich's head during his NWA World Heavyweight Championship match against Ric Flair at WCCW Christmas Star Wars 1982?

THE TERRITORIES

98. How did The Iron Sheik win the WWF Heavyweight Championship from Bob Backlund at Madison Square Garden on 26 December 1983?

99. Who was known as the 'Firebrand from the Bronx' whilst working for WWWF?

100. Charles Eugene Wolfe Jr. was the real name of which Texan wrestler, best known for his run in WCCW from 1976 until his death in 1986?

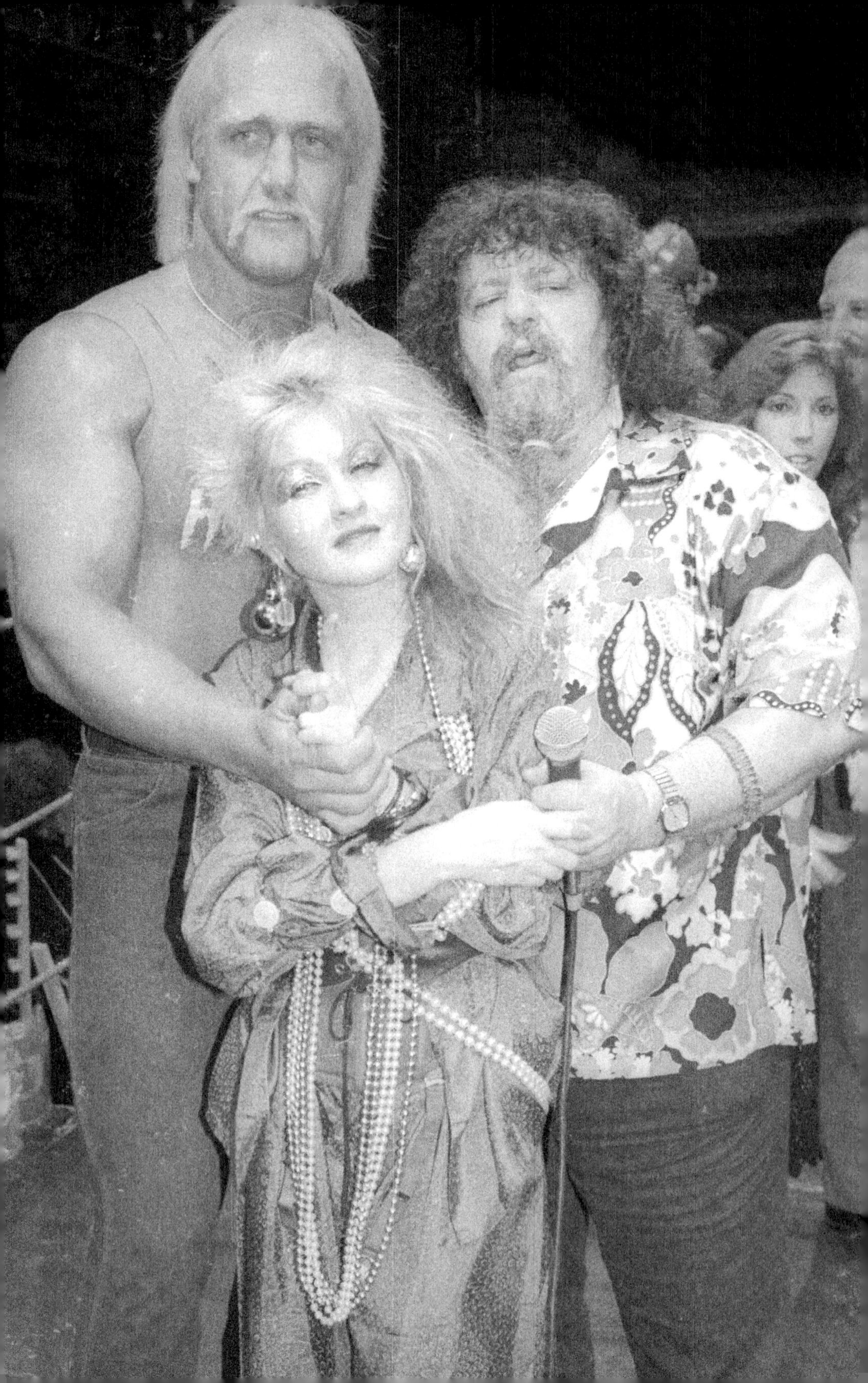

THE GOLDEN ERA

(Answers: P. 177)

1. What was the name of the first pay-per-view presented by WWF?

2. In which Cyndi Lauper music video did Lou Albano star as the artist's father?

3. Following Verne Gagne's retirement in 1981, which eloquent technician was awarded AWA's World Heavyweight Championship, a title he would go on to hold for 2,990 days across four reigns?

4. Against which comedian did Jerry Lawler wrestle at Memphis' Mid-South Coliseum on 5 April 1982?

5. Which iconic figure of Japanese wrestling won an untelevised 20-man battle royal prior to WWF's July 1984 MTV special, *The Brawl to End It All*?

6. What was the tagline of Starrcade '83, featuring Harley Race and Ric Flair's steel cage match for the NWA World Heavyweight Championship?

7. What was the name of the WWF cable television programme which premiered on USA Network in September 1983?

8. True or false? The Liberty Bell, Sears Tower, and the Golden Gate bridge all appear in the opening titles of the above programme.

THE ULTIMATE WRESTLING QUIZ BOOK

9. In March 1983, Larry Zbyszko was stripped of the NWA National Heavyweight Championship after 'buying' the title from Killer Brooks for how much?

    a) $10,000 **b)** $15,000 **c)** $20,000 **d)** $25,000

10. On 14 July 1984, Vince McMahon's WWF took over Georgia Championship Wrestling's Superstation WTBS time slot. What did this day latterly become known as?

11. Wrestler David Schultz gained widespread notoriety - but ultimately lost his job - when he did what during ABC's *20/20* special on the legitimacy of pro wrestling?

12. Ken Patera wound up with a two year jail sentence owing to a police standoff in the small hours of 6 April 1984, caused by him throwing a rock through the window of which fast-food restaurant?

13. Name the wrestler: born Patricia Seymour Schroeder on 23 January 1957 in Tampa, FL, she entered the first WrestleMania as WWF Women's Champion.

14. What colour was the WWF Intercontinental Championship held by Greg Valentine and Tito Santana throughout 1984?

THE GOLDEN ERA

15. Who did WWF hire to manage Jesse Ventura in 1984, only for the plans to be nixed when the wrestler was forced to retire due to blood clots on his lungs?

16. True or false? In March 1984, Ric Flair regained the NWA World Championship from Harley Race in a match held in Malaysia.

17. Who was Hulk Hogan a 'last-minute replacement' for in his famous WWF World Heavyweight Championship victory over the Iron Sheik in January 1984?

18. Who originally hosted *Prime Time Wrestling* alongside Jesse Ventura when the show began airing in January 1985?

19. What was pianist Liberace's role during the inaugural WrestleMania?

20. How much did Andre the Giant stand to win if he could bodyslam Big John Studd during their WrestleMania match?

21. Who did Don Muraco beat in the final to win WWF's first King of the Ring tournament, held 8 July 1985?

22. Who won the *Most Ignominious* gong at WWF's first-ever Slammy Awards, held 1986?

23. In what novel way did WWF determine the direction of Honky Tonk Man's character in 1986, following negative reactions to his babyface 'Elvis' persona?

24. True or false? WWF's '*Wrestling Bloopers, Bleeps and Bodyslams!*' was the first pro wrestling VHS released.

THE ULTIMATE WRESTLING QUIZ BOOK

25. Under what name did the wrestler, pictured below, compete when he first joined World Class Championship Wrestling in 1986?

26. In which 1986 fantasy film, starring Sean Connery, did second-generation wrestler Greg Gagne appear during the opening scene?

27. Under what military rank did Robert Remus more commonly compete?

32

THE GOLDEN ERA

28. How much did the Road Warriors claim for winning the inaugural Crockett Cup in 1986?

29. Who won the *Wrestling Observer Newsletter*'s Wrestler of the Year award five consecutive times between 1982 and 1986?

30. Who replaced Barry Windham in tag team The U.S. Express in 1986, with the duo subsequently renamed 'The American Express'?

31. From which three states did WrestleMania 2 emanate?

32. In what sort of match did Roddy Piper and Mr. T meet in the second leg of WrestleMania 2?

33. What was the name of the Miami-based spoof starring Mr. Fuji and Don Muraco, which first aired on the 7 May 1986 episode of WWF *Tuesday Night Titans*?

THE ULTIMATE WRESTLING QUIZ BOOK

34. What was the name of 'Adorable' Adrian Adonis' talk show segment, which debuted in May 1986?

35. What kick-started the WWF feud between The Islanders and The British Bulldogs in December 1987?

36. What was WWF's quoted attendance figure for 1987's WrestleMania III, held at Michigan's Pontiac Silverdome?

    a) 78,000 **b)** 80,355 **c)** 93,173 **d)** 101,763

37. Name the lawyer who represented WWF for the first time in February 1987, helping acquit Jim Neidhart of assaulting a flight attendant.

38. Which event did WWF devise to compete head-to-head with the NWA's first pay-per-view, Starrcade '87?

39. The inaugural WWF Royal Rumble was a television special aired on USA Network on 24 January 1988. Who claimed victory in the 20-man over-the-top-rope contest?

40. And what was the main event of the show?

41. "Vince McMahon made wrestling trash" - words uttered in 1989 by which former WWWF champion on the product's glamorous new direction?

THE GOLDEN ERA

42. Who did Randy Savage defeat in the semi-final of WrestleMania IV's WWF World Heavyweight Championship tournament?

43. How many seconds did it take The Ultimate Warrior to demolish Honky Tonk Man for the WWF Intercontinental Championship at SummerSlam '88?

44. What gory act by Road Warrior Animal at Starrcade '88 resulted in head booker Dusty Rhodes being fired due to the strict no-blood policy enacted by incoming owner Ted Turner?

45. Who did Rick Rude invite into the ring to kiss him on the 23 April 1988 edition of WWF *Superstars of Wrestling* - only to be refused?

46. Name the wrestler: born James Kirk Harrell on 13 December 1959 in Roanoke, VA, he is best known for his spell in WWF between 1987 and 1991.

47. The gimmick of 'Akeem, the African Dream', was created in mockery of which multiple-time NWA champion?

48. What was the finishing move of Canadian toughman Bad News Brown during his WWF tenure?

49. During his WWF stint, Dino Bravo came to the ring to the strains of *La Marseillaise*, wearing a cape patterned after the flag of Quebec. In which country was he born?

THE ULTIMATE WRESTLING QUIZ BOOK

50. Bravo was the first and only holder of which WWF championship, established August 1985 and abandoned the following January?

51. What type of technicoloured animal, named Frankie, did Koko B. Ware bring to the ring for his matches?

52. Which company's World Tag Team Championships did the wrestlers pictured below capture in a 'phantom' match following the departure of incumbent champion Steven Regal?

53. What was the name of the character portrayed by Hulk Hogan in WWF financed wrestling movie, *No Holds Barred*?

54. Which Canadian former wrestler and long-term WWE company man devised the concept of the Royal Rumble?

55. What links the WWF careers of Hulk Hogan, Iron Sheik, George Steele, Nikolai Volkoff, Adrian Adonis, and Hercules Hernandez?

56. According to the theme music of The Fabulous Rougeau Brothers, Jacques and Raymond prefer the hits of which American singer-songwriter over rock and roll?

57. What symbol did Kevin Sullivan, paint on his forehead as part of his Satanic 'Prince of Darkness' persona?

THE ULTIMATE WRESTLING QUIZ BOOK

58. Which former wrestler, more commonly found in WWF's commentary booth at the time, refereed the main event between The Mega Powers and the Mega Bucks at SummerSlam '88?

59. True or false? Hulk Hogan was in the main event of the first four WWF SummerSlam pay-per-views.

60. What is the WWF World Heavyweight Championship belt design, introduced by Hulk Hogan in 1988, more commonly known as amongst fans?

61. Jim Brunzell and B. Brian Blair formed a WWF tag team named for what winged insect?

62. With 33 million viewers tuning in, which show set a television record for American wrestling in February 1988?

63. Which of the following wrestlers is believed to have invented the 'Sharpshooter' submission hold?

    a) Bret Hart   **b)** Ronnie Garvin
    c) Riki Choshu   **d)** Sting

64. Which regular tag team wrestler defeated NWA World Heavyweight Champion Ric Flair by disqualification at Bunkhouse Stampede '88?

65. Violent tag team The Sheepherders are better known for their WWF run under what name?

THE GOLDEN ERA

66. What was the main event of the first *Clash of the Champions* television special, broadcast 27 March 1988 from the Greensboro Coliseum?

67. What did NWA stable The Four Horsemen rebrand as after appointing Hiro Matsuda as their manager in 1988?

68. Under what banner did Ted Turner originally re-incorporate WCW following his purchase of the promotion in 1988?

69. In 1988, industry outsider Jim Herd was hired as Executive Vice President of World Championship Wrestling. Which restaurant chain had he previously worked as regional manager for?

70. Herd quickly set about turning the locker room against him with various harebrained ideas for existing characters. What was the name of the Roman gimmick he pitched to company star Ric Flair, instigating 'the Nature Boy's exit?

71. On 13 December 1988, AWA staged their one and only pay-per-view event. What was it called?

72. Hulk Hogan's iconic *Real American* theme music was originally intended for which tag team?

73. Which of the following teams did *not* participate in AWA's 1989 *Team Challenge Series*, an un-aired series filmed in an empty studio featuring green-screened fans and 'foxy boxing'?

    a) Sarge's Snipers   **b)** Rheingans' Renegades
    c) Baron's Blitzers   **d)** Larry's Legends

74. At WrestleMania V, Randy Savage faced Hulk Hogan in a grudge match for the WWF World Heavyweight Championship. What was the tagline of the show?

75. True or false? Dusty Rhodes' short-term WWF manager Sapphire held a wrestling referee's license.

76. In the autumn of 1989, Rick 'The Model' Martel introduced his own brand of cologne to his WWF detractors. What was the scent called?

77. Who was the sole survivor in the 4 vs. 4 match pitting The Rude Brood against Roddy's Rowdies at Survivor Series '89?

78. Which of the following wrestlers was *not* part of the Heenan Family team which took on the Ultimate Warriors at Survivor Series '89?

    a) Bobby Heenan   **b)** Haku
    c) Arn Anderson   **d)** Tully Blanchard

79. The Ultimate Warrior and eventual winner Hulk Hogan were tied at the top of the table for most eliminations at WWF Royal Rumble '90. How many did they each manage?

80. In which Canadian stadium was WrestleMania VI held?

81. Who drove the pink Cadillac containing Rhythm & Blues to the ring at WrestleMania VI, where they debuted their new track, *Hunka Hunka Honky Love*?

THE GOLDEN ERA

82. The Ultimate Warrior retained his Intercontinental Championship when he defeated Hulk Hogan for the World title at WrestleMania VI. What was the other championship successfully defended on the show?

83. Why did 'Texas Tornado' Kerry Von Erich replace Brutus Beefcake as challenger for Mr. Perfect's WWF Intercontinental Championship at SummerSlam '90?

84. At WWF Survivor Series '90, the Gobbledy Gooker debuted to boos after hatching from an egg. Which Mexican American wrestler was under the character's turkey suit?

85. Owing to poor ticket sales, WWF moved WrestleMania VII to the Los Angeles Sports Arena, officially citing 'security concerns' over Sgt. Slaughter's Iraqi sympathiser gimmick as a reason for the switch. Where was the event originally scheduled to take place?

86. The Undertaker's much-heralded WrestleMania streak began at WrestleMania VII with victory over which wrestler?

87. How many of Randy Savage's signature elbow drops did The Ultimate Warrior survive during their WrestleMania VII retirement match?

THE ULTIMATE WRESTLING QUIZ BOOK

88. True or false? General Adnan, Sgt. Slaughter's attaché during his run as an Iraqi sympathiser, was a legitimate childhood friend of Iraqi dictator Saddam Hussein.

89. The Beverly Brothers were billed from which affluent Ohio suburb?

90. What was the name of the one-time only WWF pay-per-view held on 3 December 1991, at the end of which Hulk Hogan defeated The Undertaker for the WWF Championship?

91. Canadian heavyweight Earthquake served his patented 'Quake Burgers' to Vince McMahon, Bobby Heenan and Lord Alfred Hayes on a 1991 episode of *Prime Time Wrestling*. What meat were they made from?

92. Who was the only man to win the *Wrestling Observer Newsletter*'s now defunct Worst Wrestler of the Year award as both a WWF and WCW performer, first in 1987 and again in 1990?

93. Ric Flair claimed the WWF Championship by outlasting 29 competitors during Royal Rumble '92's eponymous event. At what number did he enter the match?

THE GOLDEN ERA

94. What act committed by Ric Flair at WrestleMania VIII saw him fined several thousand dollars by WWF after the show?

95. What piece of insider terminology was spelled out on the license plate of WWF commentator Gorilla Monsoon's sky blue Cadillac?

96. Which motoring group did the Legion of Doom's Hawk allegedly join after skipping his flight back from London following WWF SummerSlam '92?

97. Who originally partnered Bill 'Ax' Eadie as Smash in WWF tag team Demolition?

98. What was the name of the first licensed WWF video game, released on Amiga, Atari ST, Commodore 64, and DOS in 1987?

99. In which city did Bret Hart capture the WWF World Heavyweight Championship for the first time, on 12 October 1992?

100. Miss Elizabeth made her final WWF appearance at which 1992 event?

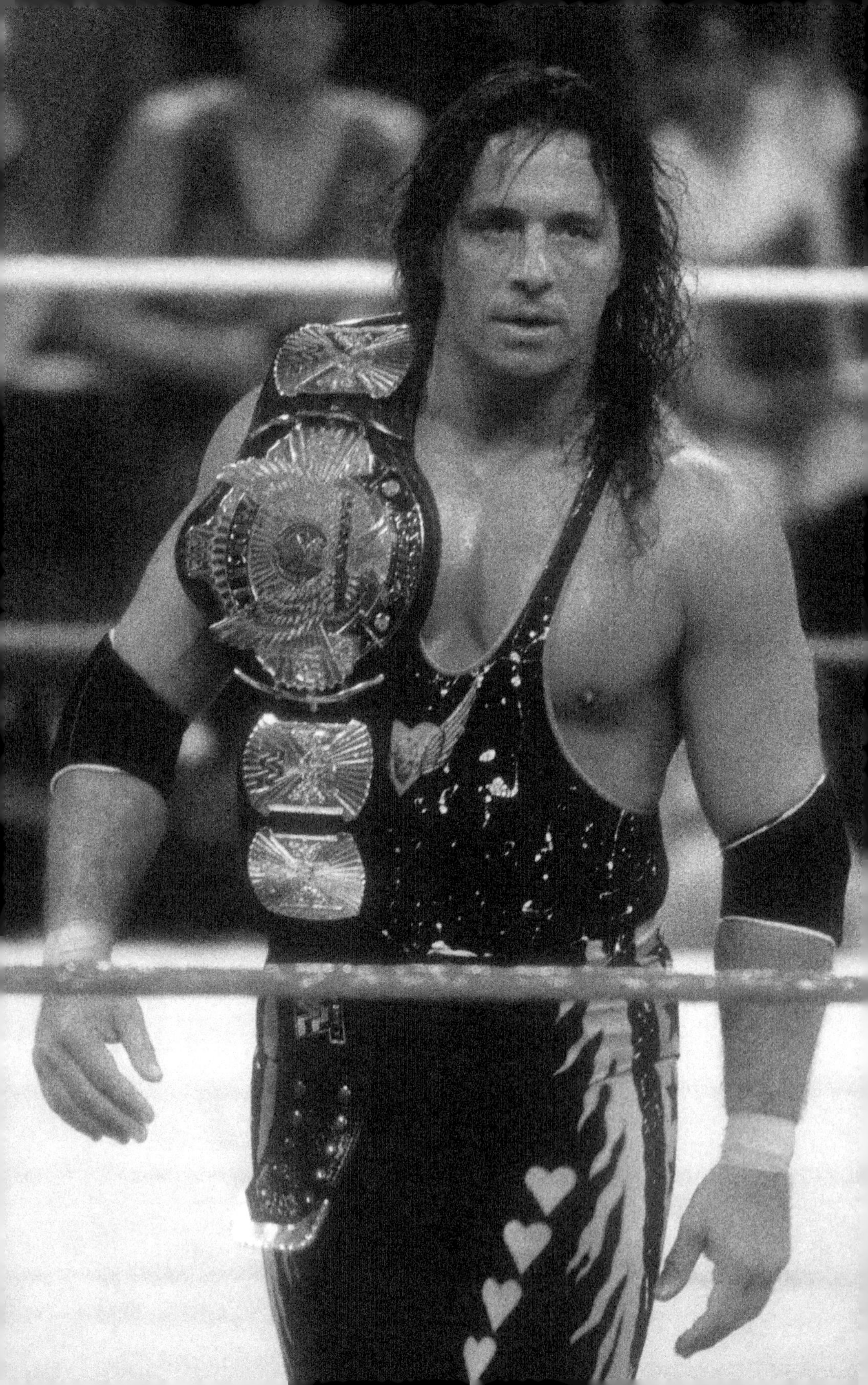

CHAPTER FOUR

A NEW GENERATION

(Answers: P. 183)

1. How many 'traditional' multi-man Survivor Series matches were part of WWF Survivor Series '92?

2. In 1992, supposed ex-sumo star Yokozuna debuted in the WWF. What does the Japanese term *'yokozuna'* mean in English?

3. On which aircraft carrier, docked in New York City, did Lex Luger bodyslam Yokozuna on Independence Day, 1993?

4. Which New York shock jock, known within the city for his radio show *Imus in the Morning*, provided *Raw* commentary duties alongside Vince McMahon and Randy Savage before being replaced by Bobby Heenan in April 1993?

5. Who did Shawn Michaels defeat to retain his Intercontinental Championship on the first episode of *Raw*?

6. How was WWF ring announcer Howard Finkel billed at the Roman themed WrestleMania IX?

7. Bobby Eaton was honoured with which rank of the nobility upon his WCW return in 1993, as part of The Blue Bloods alongside 'Lord' Steven Regal?

THE ULTIMATE WRESTLING QUIZ BOOK

8. Who did Paul Heyman replace as lead booker of Eastern Championship Wrestling in September 1993?

9. Which of the following wrestlers appeared alongside Matt Borne as the second Doink the Clown at WrestleMania IX?

   a) Dusty Wolfe   **b)** Steve Keirn
   c) Steve Lombardi   **d)** Ray Apollo

10. After WCW withdrew its membership with the NWA in September 1993, under what name was the company's 'Big Gold Belt' now promoted?

A NEW GENERATION

11. With a time of 1:01:10, which former world champion topped the charts as Royal Rumble '93's 'Iron Man'?

12. Which violent video game inspired the creation of WCW's martial arts trio of Mortis, Wrath and Glacier?

13. Who did Shane Douglas defeat in the final of ECW's NWA World Title Tournament on 27 August 1994, after which he infamously threw down the belt in an act of defiance?

14. True or false? Bam Bam Bigelow beat Tatanka to reach the final of King of the Ring '93.

15. At SummerSlam '93, The Undertaker and Giant Gonzalez met in what sort of speciality contest?

16. Which part of Native American Tatanka's Lumbee heritage did Bam Bam Bigelow steal, insitigating a feud between the pair?

17. By what term did Bam Bam Bigelow refer to his valet Luna Vachon during their association between 1992 and 1994?

18. In January 1994, Bob Holly alighted in WWF as NASCAR driver Thurman 'Sparky' Plugg. What extravagant gift did Vince McMahon give Holly to go alongside the character?

THE ULTIMATE WRESTLING QUIZ BOOK

19. How was ECW's The Sandman 'blinded' during an 'I Quit' match with Tommy Dreamer in 1994?

20. At Survivor Series '93, Yokozuna led a team of 'Foreign Fanatics' against Lex Luger's 'All-Americans' in the show's main event. Including their three managers, how many of the squad's seven men were born outside the United States?

21. At the same show, Bret Hart and his brothers Keith, Bruce, and Owen faced Shawn Michaels and a team of masked knights. Which perennial preliminary talent competed under the hood of the Red Knight?

22. True or false? More than 300,000 people - whether willingly or otherwise - attended WCW and NJPW's jointly promoted 'Collision in Korea' supershows at Pyongyang's Rungrado 1st of May Stadium across 28-29 April 1995.

23. Who won WWF's 18-man Royal Rumble, held May 1994, in Osaka, Japan?

24. To which Rocky Mountain stronghold, supposedly the lair of Big Van Vader, did Sting travel ahead of his match with the 'Mastodon' at SuperBrawl III?

A NEW GENERATION

25. Which of the following men was *not* eliminated by Diesel at Royal Rumble '94?

    a) Bart Gunn   **b)** Scott Steiner
    c) Bob Backlund   **d)** Adam Bomb

26. What popular phrase, taken from rap duo Tag Team's early-'90s hit of the same name, could often be seen emblazoned across the ring attire of Men on a Mission's Mabel?

27. Name the Japanese wrestler, noted for being the first person to spit green 'Asian mist' into his opponent's faces, who made a cameo appearance as part of Royal Rumble '94's titular match?

THE ULTIMATE WRESTLING QUIZ BOOK

28. What instrument did the WWF wrestler, pictured below, play as he made his way to the ring?

29. Name the man personally inducted into WWE's Hall of Fame by Vince McMahon in 1994, described on the company's website roll of honour as "one of the most important and influential men in sports entertainment history".

30. Based on their wrestling aliases, what qualification did Steve Williams, Slick, and Harvey Wippleman all share?

31. On 23 September 1994, promoter Herb Abrams made one last fist of his Universal Wrestling Federation promotion, with an overly ambitious show at Las Vegas' 17,000 capacity MGM Grand Garden arena. Approximately 600 punters showed up. What was the event called?

A NEW GENERATION

32. Which wrestler featured on the introduction titles for the first episode of WCW's *Monday Nitro*, but never made a single appearance on the show?

33. At which event did Hulk Hogan make his in-ring WCW debut?

34. At WrestleMania X, Leilani Kai challenged for Alundra Blayze's Women's Championship - nine years after losing the strap to Wendi Richter at the show's first edition. Which other wrestler who competed on the inaugural show made a brief appearance at the 10th outing?

35. What piece of headwear did Sly Sperling provide ring announcer Howard Finkel with at WrestleMania X?

36. What was the name of the former American footballer who could repeatedly be heard asking "What does this guy weigh?" during his guest commentary slot at King of the Ring '94?

37. Whilst WWF was promoting the 'New Generation', veterans Roddy Piper and Jerry Lawler faced off in the main event of King of the Ring '94. What was the pair's combined age?

a) 67 **b)** 75 **c)** 84 **d)** 96

THE ULTIMATE WRESTLING QUIZ BOOK

38. Which film star appeared in a number of skits investigating the disappearance and subsequent alleged sightings of The Undertaker ahead of SummerSlam '94?

39. Who replaced Samu in WWF tag team The Headshrinkers in late 1994?

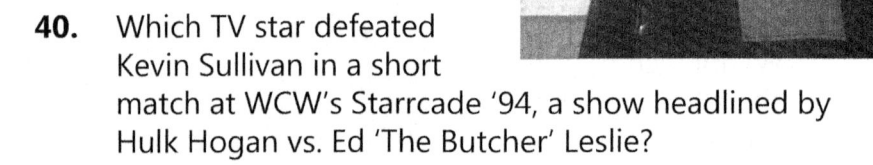

40. Which TV star defeated Kevin Sullivan in a short match at WCW's Starrcade '94, a show headlined by Hulk Hogan vs. Ed 'The Butcher' Leslie?

41. Which WCW mid-carder, who was managed by real-life cousin Colonel Robert Parker in 1994, made a 2010 appearance on WWE *SmackDown* as Jack Swagger's father?

42. Who was the only former WWF World Champion to participate in the 1995 Royal Rumble match?

43. Which English football club did Shawn Michaels surprisingly claim to be a supporter of during a Sky Sports interview in 1995?

44. On 4 September 1995, Lex Luger stunned WWF officials when he turned up on the debut episode of WCW *Nitro* at which Minnesota shopping centre?

A NEW GENERATION

45. True or false? Ludvig Borga, who chastised America for its inadequate education system and filthy environment during his mid-'90s WWE run, later became a politician for the left-leaning Social Democratic Party of Finland.

46. Which Playboy model accompanied Shawn Michaels for his WWF Championship challenge against Diesel at WrestleMania XI?

47. What was the elaborate prize for the winner of the sweepstakes WWF ran to promote the inaugural In Your House pay-per-view?

48. What gimmick was originally planned for 'Portuguese Man O' War' Aldo Montoya, only to be rejected by the wrestler himself?

49. Which rival promotion's name did disgruntled fans in Philadelphia's CoreStates Spectrum begin chanting during Mabel and Savio Vega's WWF King of the Ring '95 tournament final?

50. What unusual type of 'match' did Hulk Hogan and The Giant contest atop Detroit's Cobo Hall at WCW's Halloween Havoc '95?

51. What dramatic incident occurred after the above contest ended?

52. At WrestleMania XI, 'Supreme Fighting Machine' Kama stole The Undertaker's urn. After melting the vase down, what did he re-forge it as?

THE ULTIMATE WRESTLING QUIZ BOOK

53. In 1995, Carl Ouellet landed in the WWF as an eye-patch wearing pirate who claimed to be a direct descendant of which real-life 19th century corsair?

54. True or false? Diesel starred in the main event of the first seven WWF In Your House events.

55. Dan Spivey returned to WWF in 1995 as the soft-spoken yet sadistic Southern gentleman Waylon Mercy. From which 1991 Martin Scorsese thriller did the character draw inspiration?

56. The tag team pairing of Diesel and Shawn Michaels, which captured the WWF Tag Team Championship at In Your House 3, was collectively known as what?

57. The final episode of which long-running WWF television show aired the same day as SummerSlam '95?

58. During his first run in WWF, country music star Jeff Jarrett alleged to have released a gold record. What was it called?

A NEW GENERATION

59. What was the subtitle retroactively added to In Your House 4, held October 1995 in Winnipeg, Canada?

60. Between 1994 and 1996, Jinsei Shinzaki performed for WWF as Hakushi, a character inspired by Japanese folklore painted head-to-toe with Buddhist shakyo. What does the word 'Hakushi' mean?

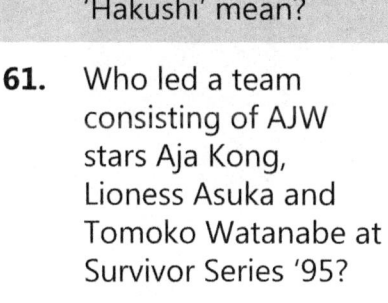

61. Who led a team consisting of AJW stars Aja Kong, Lioness Asuka and Tomoko Watanabe at Survivor Series '95?

62. Which of the following was *not* a member of Kevin Sullivan's Dungeon of Doom stable?

    a) Konnan **b)** Maxx **c)** Loch Ness **d)** Avalanche

63. Who replaced Gorilla Monsoon as WWF's on-screen president following his assault at the hands of Vader in January 1996?

64. Which of the following names was *not* pitched to Steve Austin as he sought to transition from 'The Ringmaster' moniker in 1996?

    a) Ice Dagger   **b)** Chilly McFreeze
    c) Fang McFrost   **d)** Cold Killer

THE ULTIMATE WRESTLING QUIZ BOOK

65. What was the score after 60 minutes in Bret Hart and Shawn Michaels' Iron Man match at WrestleMania XII?

66. What was the storyline daytime profession of WWF undercarder Duke Droese?

67. Under what name did future Hall of Famer Edge make his WWF debut in 1996?

68. Which German star of Hollywood's 'Golden Age of Cinema' was Goldust's cigar-smoking manager Marlena loosely based on?

69. How many tag teams did Sunny manage during her WWF stint between 1995 and 1998?

70. Which of the following men were part of Jim Cornette's 'Camp Cornette' stable?

   a) Kwang   b) Mantaur
   c) The Goon   d) Dick Murdoch

71. In Your House 8: Beware of Dog became the first WWF pay-per-view to be hosted in which state?

72. Proceedings on the 27 May 1996 episode of *Monday Nitro* were brought to a dramatic halt when Scott Hall, defecting from WWF, cleared the ring of which two competitors?

A NEW GENERATION

73. Which Bible verse did Steve Austin riff on when cutting his momentous post-King of the Ring '96 victory promo?

74. What did Brian Pillman controversially utter to end his match with Kevin Sullivan at SuperBrawl VI?

75. How many matches did The Ultimate Warrior lose during his brief WWF return in 1996?

76. True or false? Sting was originally pencilled in as the 'third man' Scott Hall and Kevin Nash would reveal at Bash at the Beach '96, prompting the formation of the New World Order.

77. Which wrestler, who captured the WWF Intercontinental Championship in 1996, had previously worked in Global Wrestling Federation under the name 'Moadib the Nubian'?

78. In a bid to reverse the losing outcome of In Your House 3's main event, Jim Cornette hired Clarence Mason as his legal counsel. Which American town was Mason billed from?

79. On 5 November 1994, ECW ran its first major show since rebranding as 'Extreme Championship Wrestling'. What was it called?

80. Name the multi-time wrestling champion who appeared in WWF under a hood as The Executioner in 1996.

THE ULTIMATE WRESTLING QUIZ BOOK

81. On 17 June 1996, WCW's *Monday Nitro* scored a ratings victory over *Raw* which kick-started 83 weeks of television dominance. What rating did *Nitro* draw that night?

    a) 2.8 b) 2.9 c) 3.0 d) 3.1

82. Name the 'futuristic' tag team made up of a second-generation wrestler and future monster truck racer, which appeared in WWF between 1995 and 1996.

83. Which ECW wrestler, alongside his manager, vaulted the guard rails during the 22 September 1996 episode of *Monday Night Raw*?

84. The Nation of Domination, formed by Faarooq in November 1996, was based on which Louis Farrakhan-led religious organisation?

A NEW GENERATION

85. In 1996, WWF hyped the debut of ex-jungle commando 'The Stalker' (in reality, Barry Windham wearing camoflague facepaint). From which vague location was he billed?

86. Who made his in-ring WWF bow at Survivor Series '96 as part of a team including Jake Roberts, Marc Mero, and The Stalker?

87. Name the wrestler: born Richard Wilson on 19 October 1965, he was best known for his WCW run as the 'Ultimate Surprise' hyped by Hulk Hogan in 1995.

88. What weapon did The Booty Man provide The Mega Powers with during their 2 vs. 8 Doomsday Cage match at Uncensored '96?

89. Which WWF belt was infamously dropped into a bin during the 18 December 1995 episode of *Monday Nitro*?

90. At which outdoor motoring event was WCW's Hog Wild held on 10 August 1996?

91. Ahead of Royal Rumble '97, WWF partnered with Mexican promotion AAA, resulting in four of the latter's roster appearing in the elimination match. Which of the following *luchadors* did *not* participate in it?

    a) Abismo Negro   **b)** Mil Máscaras
    c) Latin Lover   **d)** Pierroth

92. What were the names of the 'Funkettes' who accompanied Flash Funk to the ring during his WWF matches?

THE ULTIMATE WRESTLING QUIZ BOOK

93. On 17 February 1997, who became the first man to win WWF's top championship on an episode of *Monday Night Raw*?

94. What was the tagline of WrestleMania 13?

95. Who was Hunter Hearst Helmsley's first bodyguard, before being replaced at In Your House 13: Final Four?

96. What was the name of the disastrous nWo branded WCW pay-per-view, held 25 January 1997 at Cedar Rapids, IO's Five Seasons Center?

97. Shawn Michaels and The Undertaker's Hell in a Cell match at In Your House: Badd Blood became the second WWF match of 1997 to be awarded Dave Meltzer's coveted 5 star rating. What was the first?

98. WCW's final Clash of the Champions took place on 21 August 1997. What number was the event?

99. Who left WWF in disgust in the immediate aftermath of Survivor Series '97's infamous 'Montreal Screwjob', and as a consequence appeared on both WCW *Nitro* and a taped episode of *Monday Night Raw* on the same night?

100. Which of the following television programmes did Vince McMahon NOT liken WWF's changing product to during his landmark address on the 15 December 1997 episode of *Monday Night Raw*?

    a) Seinfeld   **b)** The Simpsons
    c) King of the Hill   **d)** Jerry Springer

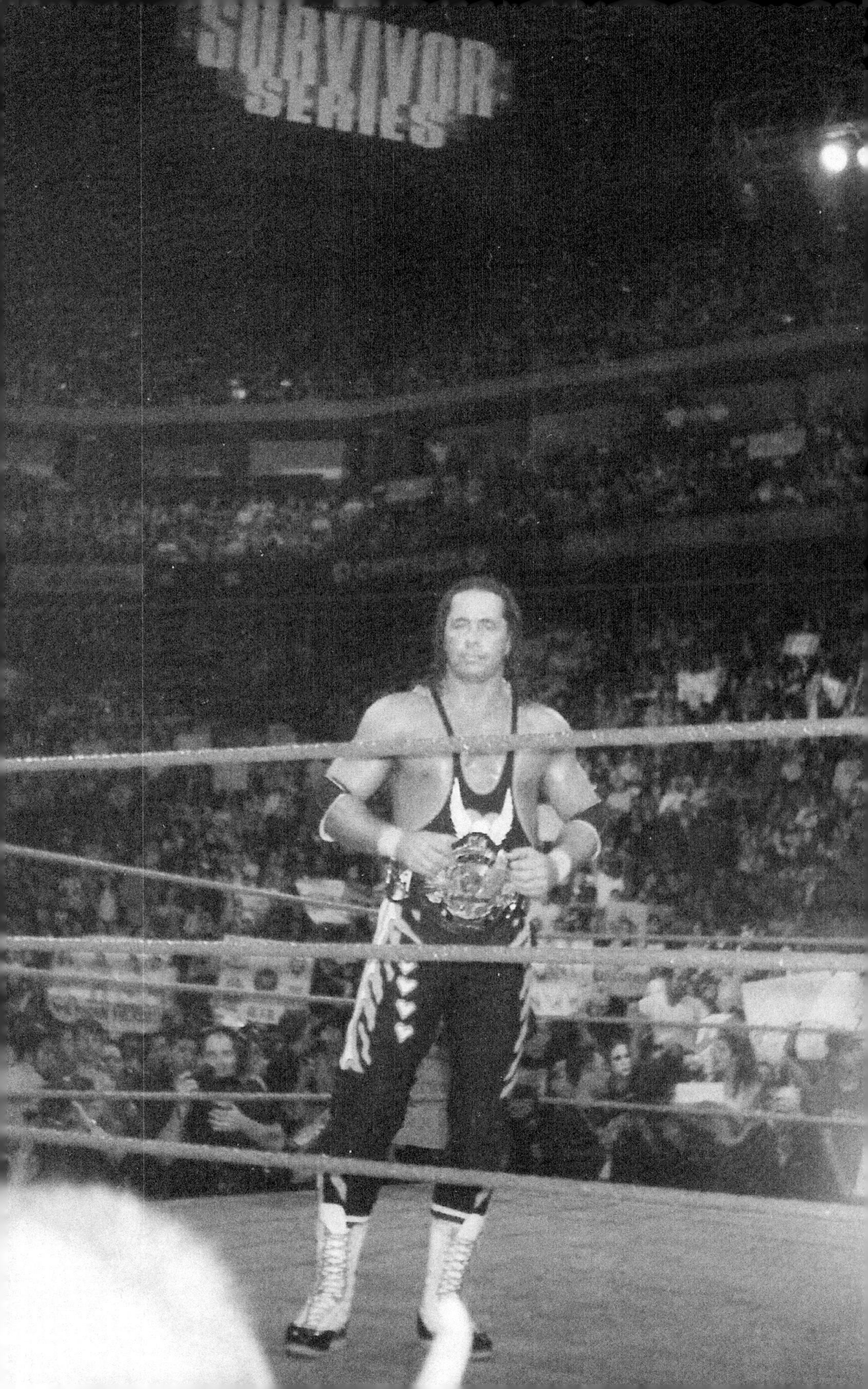
SURVIVOR
SERIES

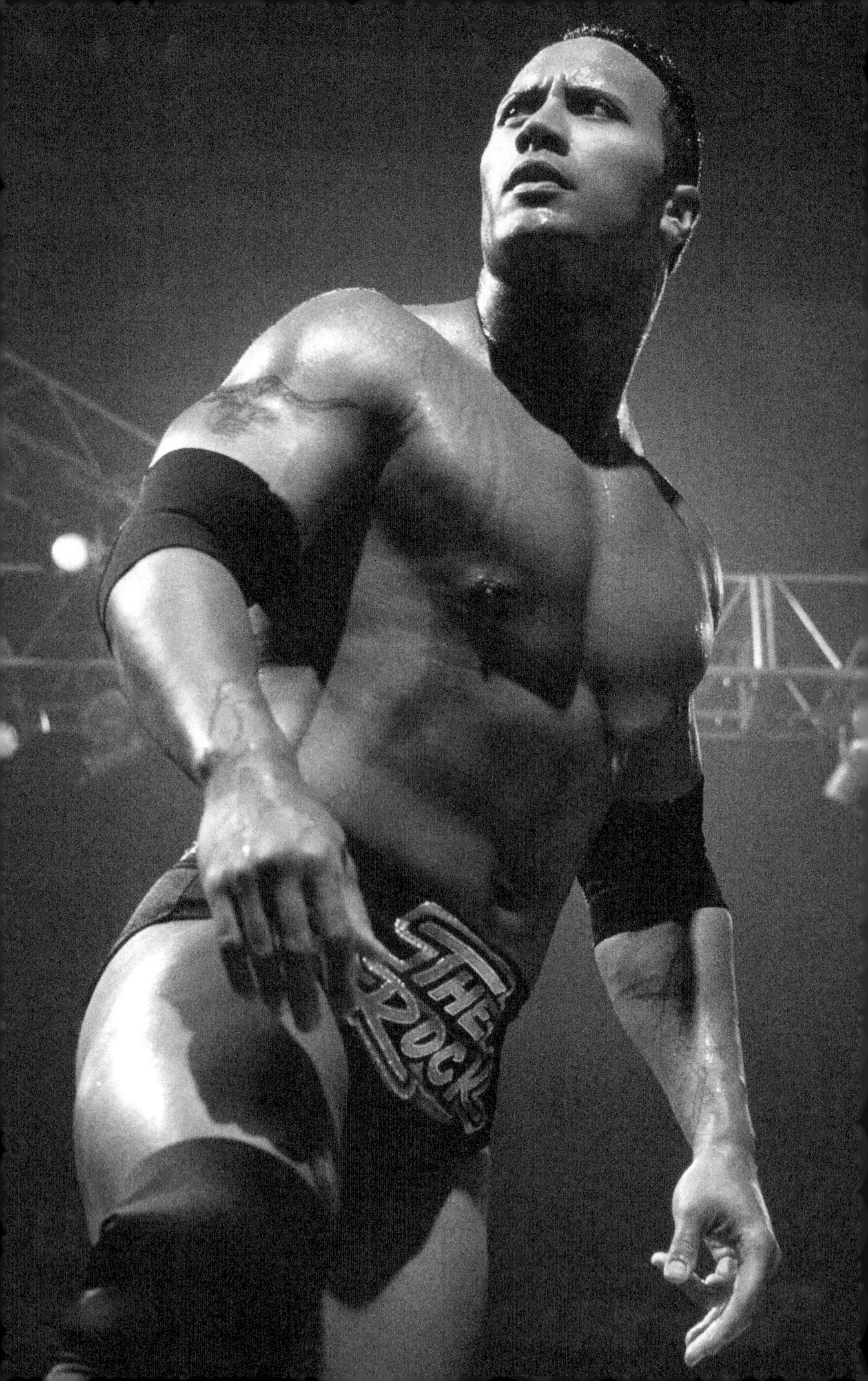
THE ROCK

CHAPTER FIVE

ATTITUDE

(Answers: P. 189)

1. Skull missed his Royal Rumble '98 slot following an attack by Los Boricuas, who had mistaken him for which superstar?

2. What was the name of the forward-thinking internet pay-per-view WCW presented on 31 January 1998?

3. What was the full title of the first No Way Out, held 15 February 1998?

4. Who replaced Shawn Michaels in the above event's non-sanctioned 8-man tag match, owing to the back injury he sustained at the previous month's Royal Rumble?

5. On 8 February 1998, WCW launched *Thunder* on TBS. What was the first match to air on the show?

6. What were the nicknames of Bob Holly and Bart Gunn during their run as an updated version of the Midnight Express in 1998?

7. In what role did Bret Hart appear at WCW Starrcade '97, just a month after joining the company from WWF?

8. What vehicle were D-Generation X driving when they invaded WCW *Nitro* at the Norfolk Scope on 27 April 1998?

THE ULTIMATE WRESTLING QUIZ BOOK

9. Which of the following people did Dustin Runnels *not* imitate during his run as 'The Artist Formerly Known As Goldust' in early 1998?

   a) Chyna **b)** Marilyn Manson
   c) Dude Love **d)** Owen Hart

10. True or false? As part of the above gimmick, Runnels considered undergoing breast implant surgery, only to be talked out of it by Vince McMahon.

11. What road sign did Raven and his flock frequently employ during their WCW incursions?

12. On 14 May 1998, ECW hosted a show coinciding with the finale of which popular American sitcom, from which it took its name?

13. Name the first move on Chris Jericho's list of 1,004 holds, reeled off on the 30 March 1998 episode of *Monday Nitro* to taunt 'Master of 1000 Holds' Dean Malenko.

ATTITUDE

14. 1998's Over the Edge: In Your House became the first WWF pay-per-view to carry which parental guidance rating?

15. From which New Mexico city were the Mick Foley personae Cactus Jack and Dude Love both billed?

16. 'Puke' was the nickname of which wrestler, who debuted as an informal member of the Legion of Doom in 1998?

17. How much did Bart Gunn win for prevailing in WWF's ill-conceived 1998 shoot-fighting tournament, the *Brawl for All*?

18. Which of the following teams did *not* appear in WrestleMania XIV's tag team battle royal?

    a) The Quebecers **b)** The Rock & Roll Express
    c) The Godwinns **d)** The New Age Outlaws

THE ULTIMATE WRESTLING QUIZ BOOK

19. In order to apologise for flirting with Yamaugchi-san's wife, Kiyogo, Val Venis presented the Kaientai manager with a preview of his latest pornographic video - in which she featured. What was it called?

20. Which member of WCW dance troupe the Nitro Girls is pictured below?

a) Chameleon **b)** Fyre **c)** Chae **d)** Tigress

21. What award was Vince McMahon presented with at the close of the 8 July 1998 episode of *Raw*?

22. Which WWF superstar demonstrated their linguistic abilities by providing Spanish commentary for the King of the Ring '98 final?

ATTITUDE

23. Golga, the masked member of eccentric WWF troupe The Oddities, would arrive to the ring clutching a soft toy of which popular cartoon character?

24. After dispensing with their 'Godwinns' moniker, what were Mark Canterbury and Dennis Knight collectively known as in WWF?

25. How much did WWF pay boxing star Mike Tyson to appear at WrestleMania XIV as a special guest referee?

26. At WCW Bash at the Beach '98, Hollywood Hogan and NBA star Dennis Rodman defeated DDP and which other basketball legend, known for his lengthy spell with Utah Jazz?

THE ULTIMATE WRESTLING QUIZ BOOK

27. The short-lived WWF tag team pairing Val Venis and The Godfather was known as what?

28. Who became WWF's first Hardcore Champion, when he was awarded the title by Vince McMahon on the 2 November 1998 episode of *Raw*?

29. Who defeated Big Boss Man in Survivor Series '98's 14-man 'Deadly Game' tournament for the vacant WWF Championship?

30. According to WCW's announcers, what was Goldberg's undefeated record before it finally ended at the hands of Kevin Nash at Starrcade '98?

31. Who was the first man to actually defeat Goldberg, in a dark match on the 24 July 1997 taping of WCW *Saturday Night*?

32. In 1999, Mick Foley released his first *New York Times* best-selling autobiography. What was it called?

33. Who holds the record for longest reign with the WWF Hardcore Championship, at 97 days?

34. In December 1998, WWF hosted a UK-only pay-per-view from Millwall's London Arena. What was the show called?

ATTITUDE

35. What was the name of the sparsely-populated stable formed by The Warrior to challenge Hollywood Hogan and the nWo?

36. A group of disgruntled WWF preliminary talents, including Al Snow and Bob Holly, banded together to form the J.O.B. Squad in November 1998. What did J.O.B. stand for?

37. Approximately how many viewers flipped from *Nitro* to *Raw* on 4 January 1999, shortly after WCW announcer Tony Schiavone revealed that Mankind was set to win WWF's top championship?

    a) 250,000 b) 500,000 c) 750,000 d) 1,000,000

38. Name the 1999 wrestling documentary movie directed by Barry Blaustein, which profiled Mick Foley, Jake Roberts and Terry Funk, amongst others.

39. Who made Royal Rumble history by earning a spot in the 1999 match through a 'Corporate Rumble' on the 11 January 1999 edition of *Raw*?

40. What sort of animal did Shane McMahon task his father Vince with catching to help him "build speed" for his upcoming appearance in the 1999 Royal Rumble?

41. What was the name of the final WWF pay-per-view officially promoted under the 'In Your House' banner, held on 14 February 1999?

THE ULTIMATE WRESTLING QUIZ BOOK

42. Tiger Ali Singh offered $500 to any American at the 7 March episode of *Sunday Night Heat* who would blow their nose on the US flag. Which Pittsburgh native in attendance pretended to accept the bait, before hitting him with a belly-to-belly suplex?

43. Into which river did The Rock throw 'Stone Cold' Steve Austin and his WWF Championship on the 12 April 1999 episode of *Raw*?

44. On 29 April 1999, WWF piloted a new wrestling show on UPN called *SmackDown*. Who provided commentary for the broadcast?

45. What was the tagline of WrestleMania XV?

46. How many seconds did it take professional boxer Eric 'Butterbean' Esch to knock out Bart Gunn in their WrestleMania XV '*Brawl for All*' contest?

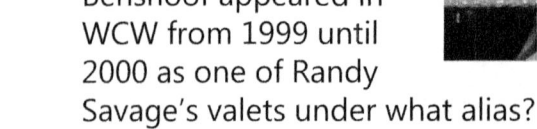

47. On the 9 August 1999 *Raw*, a promo by The Rock was dramatically interrupted by which debuting superstar?

48. Nora 'Molly Holly' Benshoof appeared in WCW from 1999 until 2000 as one of Randy Savage's valets under what alias?

49. What was unusual about the manner in which Randy Savage captured the WCW World Heavyweight Championship during Bash at the Beach '99?

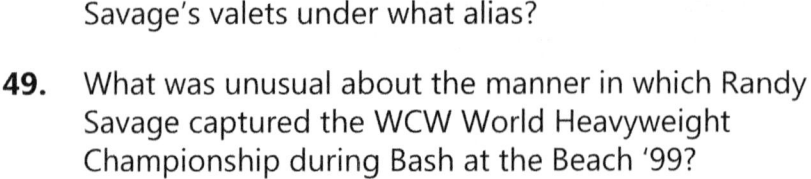

ATTITUDE

50. In mid-1999, WCW country music quartet the West Texas Rednecks hit the airwaves with their single, 'Rap is Crap'. According to the song's lyrics, who remains the king of NASCAR?

51. How many years passed between The Fabulous Moolah's first stint with the WWF (then NWA) Women's Championship, and her final run with the belt in 1999, aged 76?

52. What shrill instrument was Rob Van Dam's manager Bill Afonso frequently heard annoying crowds with during his time in ECW?

53. Who formed the ECW tag team known as the Impact Players in early 1999?

54. Which Canadian former WWF tag team champion worked several dark matches under the name (and mask) of Khris Kannonball?

55. What was the name of the Spanish-language WWF show which ran between 1998 and 1999, featuring stars from Mexican promotions AAA and CMLL as well as WWF's own lower-card talent?

56. Under what name did Shawn Stasiak wrestle in WWF as the 'boy-toy' of Terri Runnels and Jacqueline?

57. Where did Mideon find the European Championship belt on the 21 June 1999 episode of *Raw*, thus making him the champion?

58. True or false? Triple H wrestled four times on the 23 September 1999 episode of *SmackDown*.

59. Who were the three members of Shane McMahon's club of Greenwich chums, The Mean Street Posse?

THE ULTIMATE WRESTLING QUIZ BOOK

60. What was the billed weight of Bob Holly's fictional cousin 'Crash', during the pair's run as 'superheavyweights' in 1999?

61. As part of a deal that saw face-painted rock band KISS perform on the 23 August 1999 episode of *Nitro*, WCW introduced a wrestler based on the band's iconic get-up known as 'The Demon'. Which wrestler originally portrayed the character without stepping in the ring?

62. Who replaced Eric Bischoff as Senior Vice President of WCW after his effective dismissal in September 1999?

63. American bodybuilder Christi Wolfe was introduced to Shane Douglas' WCW stable The Revolution under the name 'Asya', a rib on WWF's Chyna. Under what name had Wolfe previously appeared in the company as one of Ric Flair's nurses?

64. Just one show into their deal to air WWF pay-per-views in the UK, Channel 4 were moved to delay broadcasts by 50 minutes and exercise internal editorial controls following what distasteful event at Royal Rumble 2000?

ATTITUDE

65. True or false? Kurt Angle became the first Olympic gold medallist to wrestle in WWF when he made his debut for the company at Survivor Series '99?

66. Name the former WWF pig farmer who in 2000 ditched clothes entirely and instead began streaking through the company's matches wearing nothing but a bumbag.

67. As a result of her on-screen relationship with 'Sexual Chocolate' Mark Henry, what did septuagenarian Mae Young give birth to on the 28 February 2000 episode of *Raw*?

68. What was the name of Stephanie McMahon's overzealous personal trainer, introduced on *SmackDown* in April 2000?

69. In what unhygienic way did Chris Jericho besmirch William Regal's tea on the 18 September 2000 episode of *Raw*?

70. What was unusual about the ECW World Championship match between Mike Awesome and Taz on 14 April 2000 at an Indiana house show?

71. Who faced one another in the only singles match at WrestleMania 2000?

72. After 17 years in the business, who contested their first wrestling match on 8 May 2000 against Daffney?

73. How many times did the WWF Hardcore Championship change hands during the WrestleMania 2000 battle royal for the belt?

a) 5 b) 10 c) 15 d) 20

THE ULTIMATE WRESTLING QUIZ BOOK

74. Alongside which superstar did Lita make her WWF pay-per-view debut at Backlash 2000?

75. What was the final score of the iron man match between Triple H and The Rock at Judgment Day 2000?

76. Which gold-clad duo did Edge and Christian disguise themselves as to circumvent a stipulation prohibiting them from receiving a title shot at The Hardy Boyz' tag team championship?

77. Who began what would become a glittering WWF career as the valet of tag team Test & Albert in March 2000?

78. Right To Censor, the ultra-conservative stable which protested the sexuality and violence on WWF programming, was a parody of which media advocacy group?

79. What item of clothing did Tank Abbott and Big Al fight over in their pole match at SuperBrawl 2000?

80. Which American patriot unexpectedly turned on his country to join WCW's maple-leaf flying Team Canada faction at Fall Brawl 2000?

ATTITUDE

81. Who did *Ready To Rumble* star David Arquette pin to win the WCW World Heavyweight Championship on the 25 April 2000 episode of Thunder?

82. Which WCW championship, last held by Jim Duggan after he found it in a dumpster, was retired when Vince Russo and Eric Bischoff rebooted the company in April 2000?

83. As a way to promote his upcoming *Improv All-Stars* pay-per-view, which comedian entered Royal Rumble 2001 in the number 5 position?

84. Who was the unofficial last 'holder' of WCW's Hardcore Championship, given to him by previous incumbent Meng following his departure from the company with the belt?

85. A scissor kick was the finishing move of which hulking WWF superstar, known for his time in Right to Censor?

86. What was the name of the Eric Bischoff-led group of investors who made a last ditch attempt to buy WCW, before pulling out after TimeWarner cancelled all the company's network programming?

87. How much did WWF pay for WCW's trademarks and video library, as well as the contracts of 24 talents, when the company folded in March 2001?

THE ULTIMATE WRESTLING QUIZ BOOK

88. Which of the following WCW wrestlers did Vince McMahon *not* ask the WWF crowd if they'd like to see in the company during his *Raw/Nitro* simulcast address on 26 March 2001?

   a) Lex Luger   **b)** Buff Bagwell
   c) Scott Steiner **d)** Jeff Jarrett

89. WCW effectively became defunct on 26 March 2001. Five days later, the final episode of the company's *Worldwide* television show aired. Who were the last two faces seen on WCW programming?

90. How many former WWF World Heavyweight Champions featured in WrestleMania X-Seven's tongue-in-cheek Gimmick Battle Royal?

91. What was the asset value of ECW's merchandise inventory when the company wound down in April 2001?

92. True or false? 'Gluttony' was the name of WCW's final pay-per-view event.

93. Who won the WWF Tag Team Championship alongside The Undertaker on the 18 December 2000 episode of *Raw*?

94. Alhambra Arena, Viking Hall, and 2300 Arena have all been names of the *de facto* former home venue of which wrestling organisation?

ATTITUDE

95. Which of the following were *not* members of the nWo's NJPW branch, nWo Japan?

   a) Yuji Nagata   **b)** Satoshi Kojima
   c) Masa Chono   **d)** Scott Norton

96. Swoll, Chase Tatum, and 4x4 were all members of which WCW faction?

97. Who tagged with AJ Styles on *Thunder* during the tail end of WCW's time in business?

98. Name the wrestler: born 26 April 1967 in Torrejon de Ardoz, Spain, he competed in the early part of his career as Angus King and Spartacus.

99. In which UK city was WWF's 2000 pay-per-view Rebellion held?

100. Which American thrash metal band provided the opening theme of WCW *Thunder, Here Comes the Pain*?

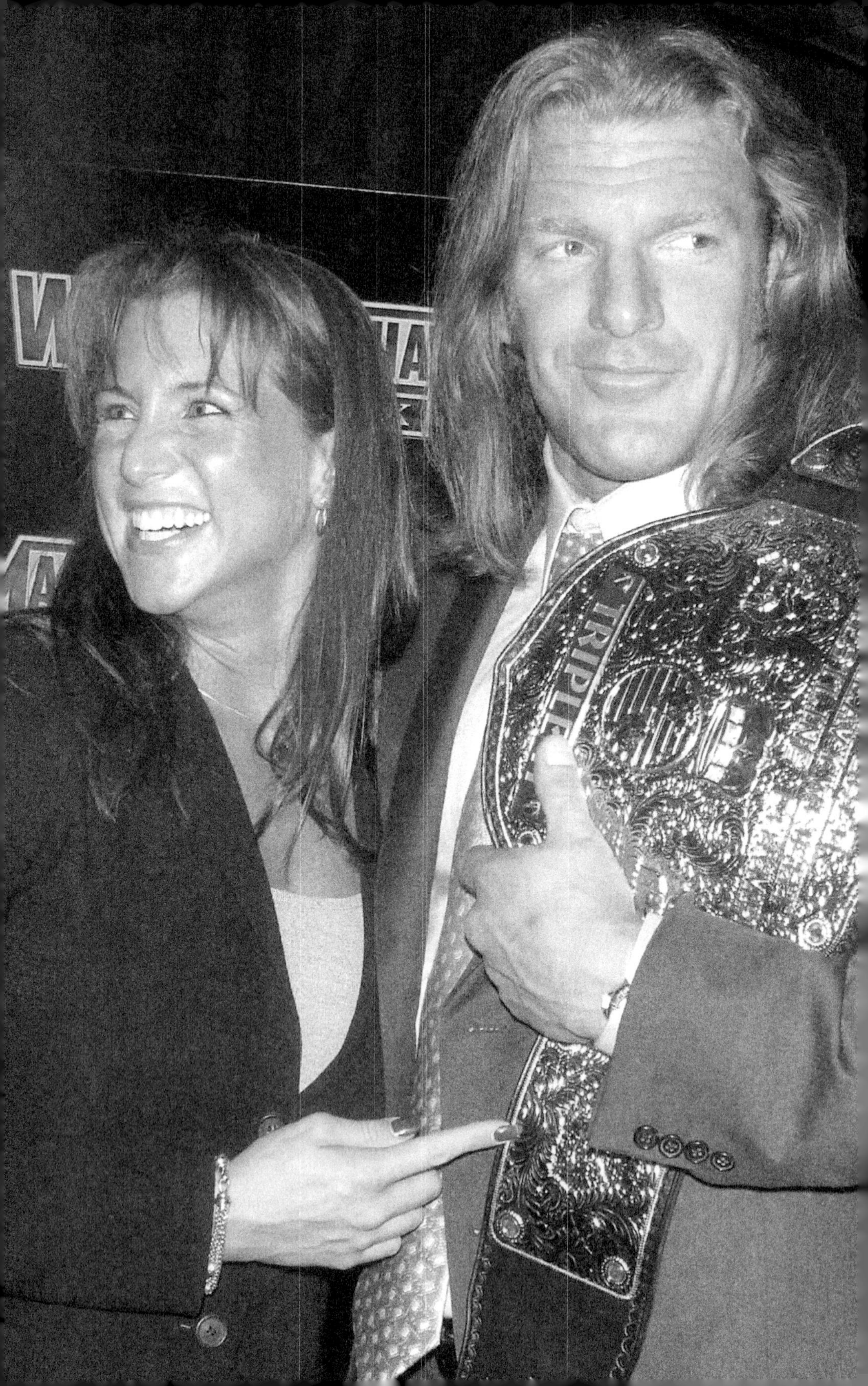

CHAPTER SIX

THE MONOPOLY

(Answers: P. 195)

1. True or false? Jeff Jarrett was legitimately fired from WWF by Vince McMahon on the 26 March 2001 episode of *Raw*, after the chairman stated on air that Double J was "g-o-double n-e".

2. Following their purchase of WCW, WWF rebranded the last portion of the 2 July 2001 episode of *Raw* under the WCW name, during which Buff Bagwell and Booker T wrestled before jeers from the WWF crowd. What was the commentary team for the match?

3. Who injured 'Stone Cold' Steve Austin within seconds of making his WWF debut by throwing him through a table at King of the Ring 2001?

4. Popular WCW babyface and future motivational speaker-cum-fitness instructor Diamond Dallas Page was bizarrely introduced to WWF as the stalker of The Undertaker's wife. What was her name?

5. Which legendary WWF manager gave a rousing speech to the company's assembled forces on the 16 July 2001 *Raw*, ahead of the WWF vs. WCW/ECW 'Inaugural Brawl' at InVasion?

6. Which team did The Brothers of Destruction defeat at Unforgiven 2001, with the match later earning the *Wrestling Observer*'s ignominious 'Worst Worked Match of the Year' award?

THE ULTIMATE WRESTLING QUIZ BOOK

7. Who featured on the poster for Survivor Series 2001, headlined by a 'winner takes all' 5-on-5 Survivor Series match between Team WWF and The Alliance?

8. Under what name did Josh Lomberger, a runner-up in the first season of WWF reality contest *Tough Enough*, eventually work for the company?

9. Triple H was placed on the poster for which 2001 WWF pay-per-view - despite not participating in the show?

10. The World Wrestling Federation was rebranded as 'World Wrestling Entertainment' on 6 May 2002 following a protracted legal battle over a trademark with which conservation organisation?

11. True or false? The concept of TNA was devised whilst Jerry Jarrett, his son Jeff, and digital wrestling pioneer Bob Ryder were away on a motorcycling trip.

12. In what liturgical capacity did Batista make his WWE debut alongside 'Reverend' D-Von in May 2002?

13. The 'TNA Asylum', at which the majority of TNA's weekly pay-per-views were hosted, is officially known as what?

THE MONOPOLY

14. How many weekly pay-per-views did TNA host before presenting their first three-hour, monthly pay-per-view?

15. Who made an OVW appearance in November 2001 under the name 'Mr. P', as part of a six-man tag match with Big Boss Man and Charlie Haas?

16. Which of the following was *not* part of WWE's incarnation of the New World Order?

    a) Booker T **b)** Big Show
    c) Shawn Michaels **d)** Scott Steiner

17. How old was Hulk Hogan when he captured the WWF Undisputed Championship at Backlash 2002?

18. In what manner did Triple H claim WWE's newly-minted World Heavyweight Championship on the 2 September 2002 edition of *Raw*?

19. Which secondary championship became exclusive to the *Raw* brand when the incumbent champion was drafted to the show during the first WWE Draft Lottery in May 2002?

THE ULTIMATE WRESTLING QUIZ BOOK

20. Shawn Michaels made his return to WWE at SummerSlam 2002, taking on former stable-mate Triple H in an unsanctioned street fight. For which Texas-based promotion did Michaels interrupt his wrestling hiatus in April 2000, working a hardcore match with Paul 'Venom' Diamond?

21. By what acronym did 'WWE superhero' Hurricane Helms refer to his sidekick, Rosey?

22. At the tender age of 25, Brock Lesnar broke the record of WWE's youngest world champion in defeating The Rock at SummerSlam 2002. Who had previously been the company's youngest top champion?

23. The group of technically proficient wrestlers comprised of Chris Benoit, Edge, Eddie Guerrero, Kurt Angle, Rey Mysterio, and Chavo Guerrero were known amongst wrestling fans as what?

THE MONOPOLY

24. Shortly after Vince McMahon told Hulk Hogan he would have to sit out the remainder of his WWE contract in 2003, a mysterious masked superstar with a golden mustache known as 'Mr. America' made his debut. Which of the following wrestlers did *not* appear on a WWE.com poll asking fans about his possible identity?

    a) Mark Henry   b) Mr. Fuji
    c) Bastion Booger   d) Nailz

25. Who stabbed John Cena in a nightclub at the behest of rival Carlito Carribbean Cool as part of a 2004 *SmackDown* storyline?

26. In what unusual way were the matches at WWE's October 2004 pay-per-view Taboo Tuesday decided?

27. How many rules originally made up Ring of Honor's 'Code of Honor', a set of tenets by which the promotion's wrestlers were expected to abide?

28. True or false? Shelton Benjamin competed in the Men's Greco-Roman Wrestling discipline at the 2000 Summer Olympics in Sydney.

29. What high-risk manoeuvre did Brock Lesnar spectacularly botch during the closing stages of his WrestleMania XIX clash with Kurt Angle?

30. The Undertaker was accompanied to his WrestleMania XIX handicap match against A-Train and Big Show by which Australian former powerlifter?

THE ULTIMATE WRESTLING QUIZ BOOK

31. Rodney Mack and Christopher Nowinski were part of which Theodore Long-led stable?

32. Rico Constantino, Chuck and Billy's one-time personal stylist, won WWE tag team gold on two occasions with two different partners in the company. Who were they?

33. At which show did WWE debut the Elimination Chamber gimmick match?

34. True or false? *Tough Enough* Season 1 runner-up and brief WWE competitor Christopher Nowinski graduated from MIT with a BA in Sociology.

35. At WrestleMania XX, two wrestlers became the first born in the 1980s to compete at WWE's showcase event. Who were they?

36. At which New York hotel was WWE's 2004 Hall of Fame ceremony hosted?

37. True or false? Randy Orton became the first third-generation wrestler to win one of WWE's top championships when he defeated Chris Benoit for the World Heavyweight Championship at SummerSlam '04.

38. Who was the only man to defeat Goldberg in singles competition during his first WWE run between 2003 and 2004?

THE MONOPOLY

39. Which WCW pay-per-view did WWE revive in June 2004?

40. What happened to The Undertaker's manager Paul Bearer at the end of The Great American Bash 2004?

41. What was the name of WWE's developmental territory between 2000 and 2008?

42. Which star of WWE's 'Ruthless Aggression' era had previously tried out at WCW's Power Plant training school, only to be told by trainer DeWayne Bruce that he would never make it in the business?

43. Evolution, a modern-day interpretation of The Four Horsemen, was fomed in 2003. Who was originally in line to join leader Triple H, Ric Flair, and Randy Orton in the group?

44. In 2004, Bradshaw was repackaged as 'JBL', a J.R. Ewing-esque business tycoon inspired by his real-life position as a financial analyst for which American news channel?

45. Who failed to enter Royal Rumble 2005 after being attacked by Muhammad Hassan on the way to the ring?

46. True or false? Batista and John Cena's double-elimination at the end of the 2005 Royal Rumble match was a legitimate botch; Batista was not supposed to hit the floor.

THE ULTIMATE WRESTLING QUIZ BOOK

47. Kenzo Suzuki's geisha Hiroko and Torrie Wilson took part in a match on the 10 February 2005 episode of *SmackDown*, with the aim being to strip the opponent of what item of clothing?

48. Which of the following wrestlers was *not* involved in the six-pack challenge for Funaki's Cruiserweight Championship at No Way Out 2005?

    a) Juventud   **b)** Akio
    c) Chavo Guerrero   **d)** Paul London

49. At WrestleMania 21, Edge became the first man to win WWE's Money in the Bank ladder match. At which show did he successfully cash in his contract?

50. What was unusual about the match line-up for WrestleMania 21?

51. Under what ring name was Low Ki competing when he won TNA's X Division Championship from Samoa Joe in June 2006?

52. What was the title of the choleric poetry recited by Heidenreich during his heel spell under the direction of Paul Heyman?

53. The Mexicools trio of Juventud Guerrera, Super Crazy, and Psicosis made their way to ring astride what type of vehicle?

THE MONOPOLY

54. True or false? The Great Khali, around whom the 'Punjabi Prison' cage match was devised, used to work as an officer for the Punjab Police.

55. Which two superstars featured in the first version of the above match type, held at Great American Bash 2006?

56. Who became Booker T's 'Queen' following his King of the Ring 2006 victory?

57. Which WWE superstar did the future Doc Gallows pose as during his 2005 spell in the promotion?

58. Which wrestling manager made his one and only WWE appearance at the company's ECW revival One Night Stand?

THE ULTIMATE WRESTLING QUIZ BOOK

59. The creepy, gyrating WWE horror known as The Boogeyman would often stuff which squirming, live creature into his mouth?

60. In April 2005, TNA launched a pay-per-view on which every match would take place within the confines of a steel cage. What was it called?

61. Which character did television network UPN demand WWE remove from their programming, after his on-screen actions drew parallels to the real-life tragedy of the 2005 London bombings?

62. What was the name of Tatanka's new finisher - the Lakota word for 'thunder' - following his WWE return in 2005?

63. Belfast-born bruiser Finlay was commonly seen brandishing what weapon, its name an Irish term meaning 'thonged willow'?

64. Following an earlier run as Eric Bischoff's hired muscle Jamal, Edward Fatu returned to WWE in December 2005 as the 'Samoan Bulldozer' Umaga. What does the word 'Umaga' - which derives from the painful traditional Samoan tattoo process - mean?

THE MONOPOLY

65. On 1 October 2005, TNA launched a weekly TV show on cable network Spike TV. What was the show called?

66. Which match at TNA's Unbreakable pay-per-view in 2005 became the only one in company history to receive a five-star rating from the *Wrestling Observer*'s Dave Meltzer?

67. What is the name of the 2007 action film produced by WWE starring 'Stone Cold' Steve Austin and former footballer Vinnie Jones?

68. At Backlash 2006, Vince & Shane McMahon faced Shawn Michaels and 'God'. 'God's theme music was previously used by which dancing WWE star?

69. On 3 December 2006, the WWE-presented ECW December to Dismember pay-per-view drew the lowest buyrate in the company's history. Approximately how many people purchased the show?

    a) 10,000 **b)** 40,000 **c)** 90,000 **d)** 120,000

70. Name the six men who competed in ECW's one and only Elimination Chamber match at the above event.

71. What was the peculiar objective of the battle royal portion of TNA's 2006 Fight for the Right tournament?

THE ULTIMATE WRESTLING QUIZ BOOK

72. Of the nine men inducted into the 2007 WWE Hall of Fame, how many were former WWE World Champions?

73. Which body part did WWE's former baby-punter Snitsky have to regularly discolour as part of his new 'psychotic' persona in 2007?

74. Whilst wrestling as Matt Hardy Version 1, various facts about Hardy's life would appear on screen during his entrances. Which of the following is *not* a genuine 'Matt Fact'?

   a) Matt strongly dislikes mustard.
   b) Matt has been to Plymouth Rock.
   c) Matt has a heated toilet seat.
   d) Matt can speak conversational Spanish.

THE MONOPOLY

75. Having vanquished The Spirit Squad in a 5 vs. 3 handicap match on the 27 November 2007 episode of *Raw*, DX threw all the members of the troupe into a crate stamped for what destination?

76. In TNA's 'Feast or Fired' match, the company's spin on WWE's Money in the Bank concept, three of the four potential briefcases contained title shots. What booby prize was in the fourth?

77. Throughout 2007, Jillian Hall began serenading audiences with her singing - oblivious to the fact it was terrible. That Christmas, WWE released a parody album of her music known as what?

78. True or false? The above record sold more copies than Brooke Hogan's debut album, *Undiscovered*.

79. Name the wrestler: born Chadwick Rowan on 8 May 1969, he made his sole televised appearance in WWE at WrestleMania 21, and later had spells in NJPW, Dragon Gate, and Hustle.

80. TNA's musical trio of Lance Rock, Jimmy Rave, and Christy Hemme were known as what?

81. WWE tag team The Heart Throbs was made up of which two wrestlers?

82. In June 2007, a team of backwoods hillbillies known as Jesse and Festus alighted on *SmackDown*. Which acclaimed wrestler was the father of Jesse?

THE ULTIMATE WRESTLING QUIZ BOOK

83. Who ended Chris Masters' 'Masterlock Challenge' two years after it had first commenced when he broke from the hold on the 20 March 2007 episode of *Raw*?

84. As a nod to the Fantastic Four film released that year, which Marvel superhero did Rey Mysterio dress as for his match with Chavo Guerrero at SummerSlam 2007?

85. Who was the final holder of WWE's original Cruiserweight Championship when it was unofficially deactivated in September 2007?

86. True or false? John Cena headlined eight pay-per-views in a row in 2007, starting with No Way Out (with Shawn Michaels vs. The Undertaker and Batista) and ending with SummerSlam (vs. Randy Orton).

87. True or false? WrestleMania 23, which featured a 'Battle of the Billionaires' between businessmen Vince McMahon and Donald Trump, was the 5th time the 45th President of the United States had appeared at WrestleMania.

88. What baseball term links the WWE gimmicks of Steve Lombardi and Hassan Assad?

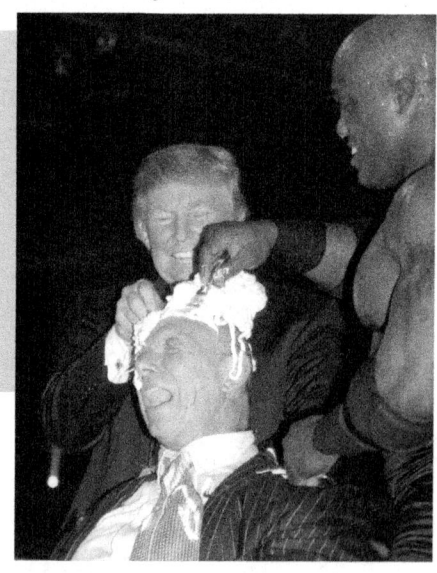

89. What was the name of the rollerskating WWE Diva who accompanied greaser duo Deuce 'n' Domino for their matches?

90. True or false? Christian wrestled for NJPW in 2008.

THE MONOPOLY

91. Which R&B singer, once of Destiny's Child, performed a rendition of *America the Beautiful* at WrestleMania 22?

92. What chance of beating Samoa Joe at TNA's Sacrifice 2008 did Scott Steiner calculate for himself during a memorable mathematics-laden promo?

93. Who held the Ring Of Honor World Championship for 462 days between 17 September 2005 and 23 December 2006?

94. Before Sweet Chin Music-ing Ric Flair into retirement at WrestleMania XXIV, what sentimental words did Shawn Michaels mouth to the outgoing legend?

95. On 4 April 2008, Ukrainian brute Vladimir Kozlov made his WWE debut with a squash against Matt Bentley. What was unusual about his entrance?

THE ULTIMATE WRESTLING QUIZ BOOK

96. From 2008, Vengeance became known by what name, previously the subtitle of the 2007 edition?

97. What was the name of the competition WWE devised in 2008, during which the company legitimately gave away $1 million in a desperate bid to drum up fresh interest in *Raw*?

98. Vince McMahon was greeted to the sound of which 1987 pop hit (and later internet meme) during his bungled attempts to call a contestant of the above contest on the 10 June 2008 episode of *Raw*?

99. What was Triple H's prison number on the poster of Judgment Day 2008?

100. What significant change to WWE's programming made in July 2008 did company CEO Linda McMahon describe as a 'cradle-to-the-grave approach' for attracting viewers?

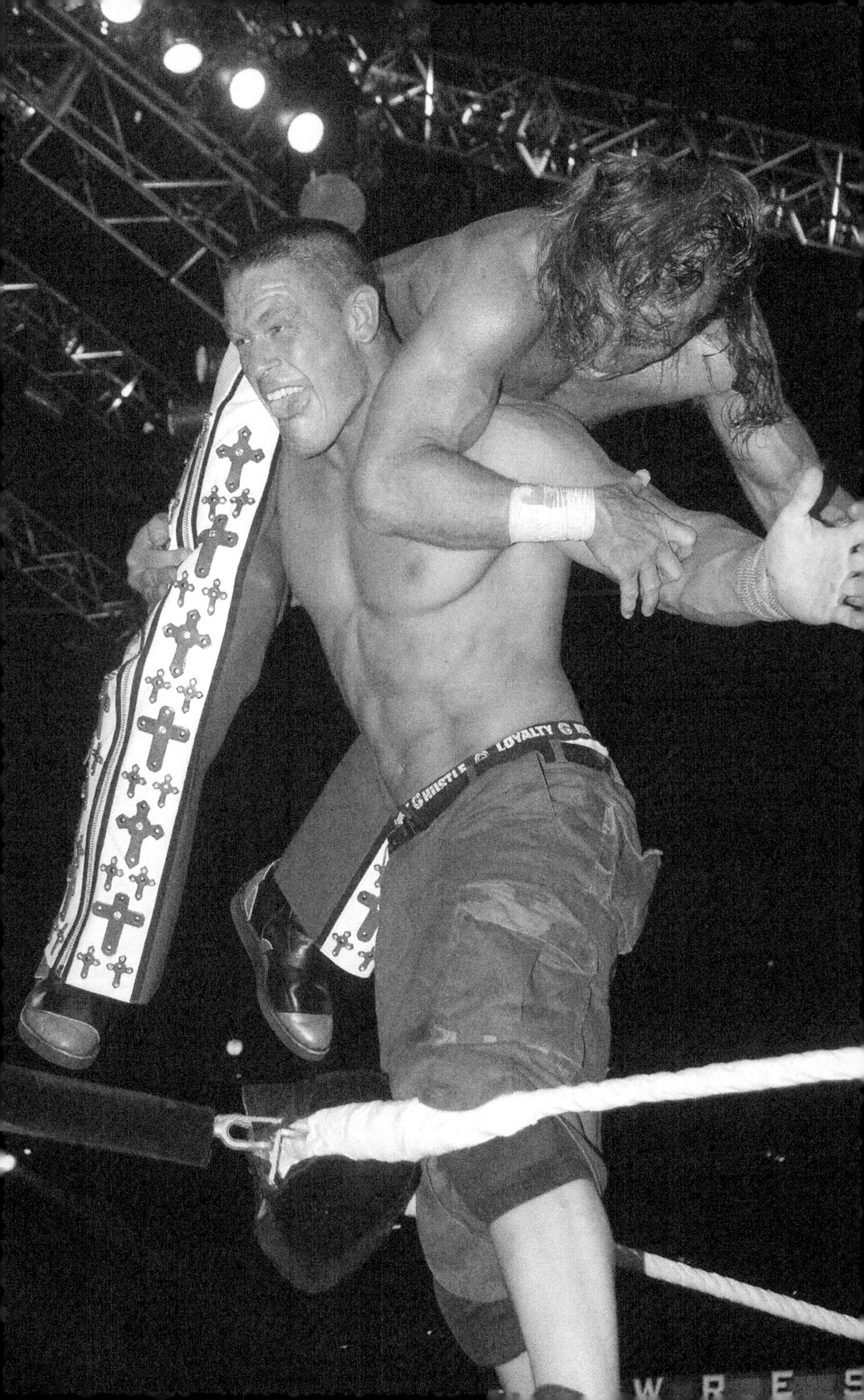
LOYALTY
HUSTLE
LOYALTY
W R E S

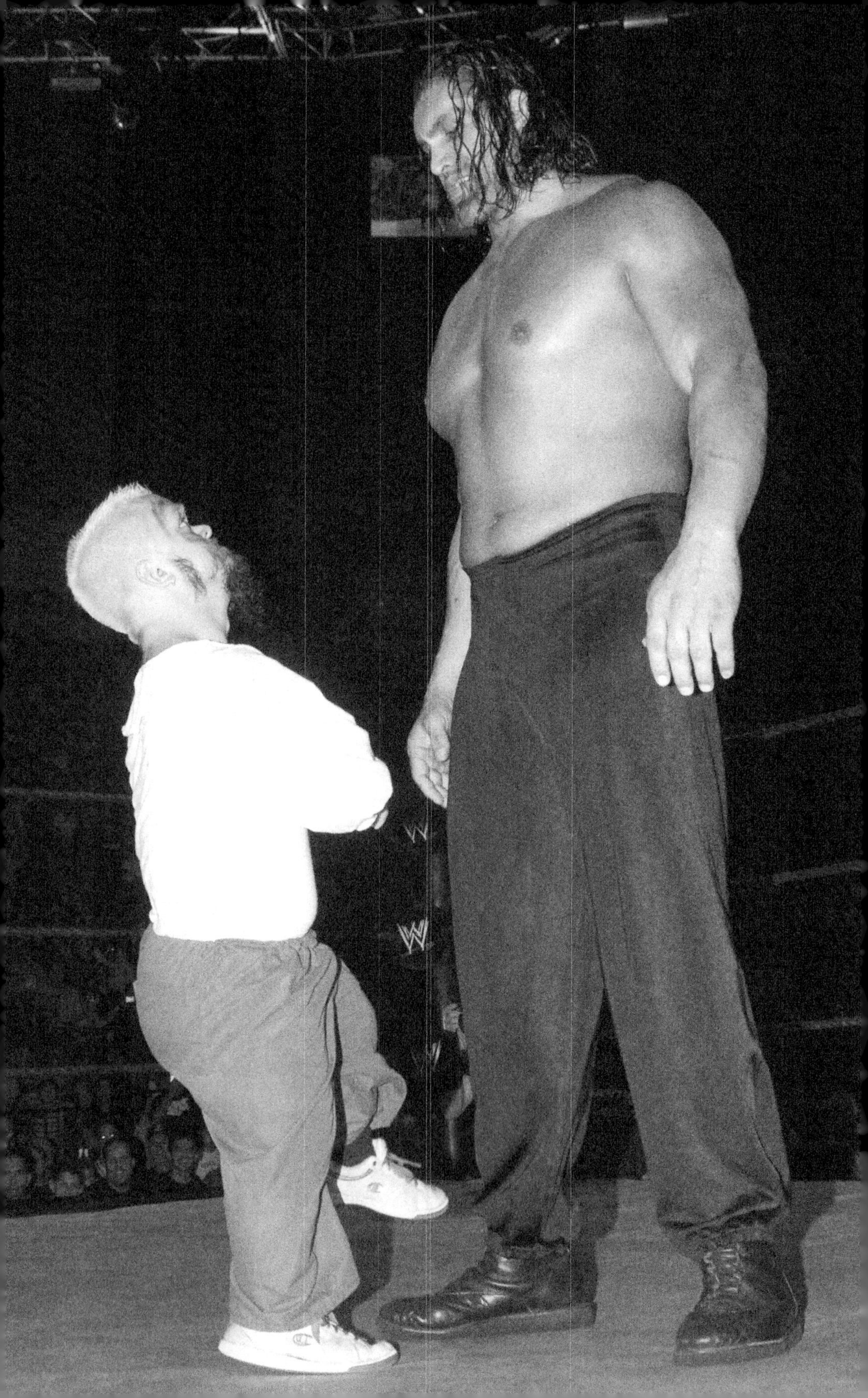

CHAPTER SEVEN

THE PG ERA

(Answers: P. 201)

1. Which beloved wrestler and commentator was Santino Marella named in homage of?

2. Whose lip did Chris Jericho legitimately accidentally bust during a SummerSlam 2008 angle?

3. The poster for Unforgiven 2008 featured a rain-soaked Batista in reference to an iconic scene from which 1995 movie?

4. Cryme Tyme's JTG came up with his name after telling himself during developmental that he was 'just too good'. What did the wrestler tell WWE officials it stood for, in order to avoid any backstage heat?

5. Which former WWE Tag Team Champion began managing Mark Henry in the summer of 2008?

6. *The Dirt Sheet*, an online show which mocked wrestlers and popular culture, was hosted by which two superstars?

7. Which video game character did Mickie James dress as to win Cyber Sunday's fan-voted Divas Halloween costume contest?

8. How many casket matches did The Undertaker win in 2008?

THE ULTIMATE WRESTLING QUIZ BOOK

9. Sho Funaki began wrestling in WWE under his 'full name' in October 2008, revealed to R-Truth in a backstage skit as what?

10. After which two former US Presidents was a WWE ECW wrestler/interviewer, real name Brian Jossie, named?

11. What was the name of the fictional professional wrestler portrayed by Mickey Rourke in Darren Aronofsky's critically acclaimed 2008 film?

12. What genealogical fact linked the three members of WWE faction Legacy?

13. Name the match between a TNA Knockout and a former Survivor contestant at Victory Road 2009 that was 'awarded' a minus 5-star rating by the *Wrestling Observer*'s Bryan Alvarez?

14. What storyline 'accident' afflicted Jeff Hardy during his entrance on the 16 January 2008 episode of *SmackDown*, later revealed to be a deliberate ambush by brother Matt?

15. Who did Vince McMahon introduce as a "future world champion" on the 25 October 2009 episode of *SmackDown*?

16. Who was the only unbranded participant in the Royal Rumble 2009 match?

THE PG ERA

17. 'Sliced Bread #2' was the finishing move of which WWE cruiserweight?

18. True or false? Kofi Kingston was the second African-born wrestler to perform in WWE, after Kamala.

19. Santino Marella broke The Warlord's ignominious record for shortest stint in the Royal Rumble match following his elimination by Kane at the 2009 event. How long did he last?

20. Short-lived WWE gimmick Kizarny was named for which slang patois, first used by itinerant showmen and later adopted by the wrestling industry?

21. What was the storyline former profession of La Famillia bodyguard Bam Neely?

22. Which of the following competed in No Way Out 2009's *Raw* Elimination Chamber?

    a) Jack Swagger   b) Mike Knox
    c) Randy Orton   d) Shane McMahon

23. A tag team match to unify the championships of *Raw* and *SmackDown* (The Miz & John Morrison vs. The Colons) was bumped to the WrestleMania 25 pre-show to make way for a performance by which musician?

THE ULTIMATE WRESTLING QUIZ BOOK

24. How old was Jimmy Snuka at WrestleMania 25 when he became the oldest person to wrestle at the flagship event?

25. For what honour did Santino Marella and Chavo Guerrero wrestle a Handicap Hog Pen Match at Extreme Rules 2009?

26. In 2010, TNA changed the name of regular pay-per-view Hard Justice to 'Hardcore Justice', converting the card into an ECW tribute show. What was the name of the supplementary Impact special held the next night which featured Hardcore Justice's original line-up?

27. What was The Great American Bash rebranded as for the 2009 event?

28. Which star of the 2010s independent scene became the youngest person ever signed to a WWE developmental contract when he joined the company in 1998?

29. On which MTV reality show did The Miz first gain fame before earning a WWE contract through *Tough Enough*?

30. What insect was depicted in pink rhinestones as part of the WWE Divas Championship's patronising title belt design?

31. What did comedian Jeremy Piven repeatedly call SummerSlam whilst promoting the show on the 3 August 2009 episode of *Raw*?

100

THE PG ERA

32. Name the wrestler: born Zivile Raudoniene in Alytus, Lithuania, she married Goldust in a WWE storyline in order to obtain a US green card.

33. True or false? Between 1989 and 2010, the Million Dollar Championship was awarded to a wrestler more times than it was won in a match.

34. Who was the final General Manager of WWE's ECW brand before it was discontinued in 2010?

35. How many Hell in a Cell matches featured on the first Hell in a Cell pay-per-view in October 2009?

36. What was the motto of NXT breakout faction The Nexus under the leadership of CM Punk?

37. What was the final score between the brands of *SmackDown* and *Raw* at Bragging Rights 2009?

38. True or false? Every member of the Hart Dynasty was a direct descendant of Hart family patriarch Stu Hart.

39. Former Spirit Squad cheerleader Nicky returned to *Raw* on the 15 September 2008, repackaged as 'Showoff' Dolph Ziggler. What was his name originally intended to be?

40. Which legendary WWE commentator returned to the announce desk for the episode of *Raw* the night after Survivor Series '09?

THE ULTIMATE WRESTLING QUIZ BOOK

41. Which set of tag teams started an on-screen romantic relationship on *SmackDown* in November 2009?

42. At which UK venue in January 2009 did a house show headlined by Jeff Jarrett vs. Kurt Angle set an all-time TNA record attendance of 8,100?

43. True or false? Every member of Team Miz at Survivor Series 2009 was a future WWE World Champion.

44. Who eliminated The Great Khali at Royal Rumble 2010?

45. How did TNA alter their ring configuraiton at Genesis 2010?

46. What sort of animal did Chavo Guerrero portray as Jack Swagger's mascot in 2010, a rib on his uncle donning a similar costume at Survivor Series '90 nearly 20 years earlier?

47. Who became the first man to appear in Royal Rumbles in the '80s, '90s, '00s and '10s with his appearance in Royal Rumble 2010's titular match?

48. Which of the following did *not* make their TNA debut on 4 January 2010, the night *Impact!* began going head-to-head with WWE *Raw* on Mondays?

    a) Hulk Hogan   **b)** Ric Flair
    c) Eric Bischoff   **d)** Jeff Hardy

49. Meanwhile, which two embittered superstars finally buried the hatchet on-screen on the night's opposing *Raw*?

THE PG ERA

50. True or false? Despite losing heavily to *Raw* in the ratings, the 4 January 2010 *Impact!* was the most viewed episode in TNA history.

51. In 2009, Bryan Danielson was named the *Wrestling Observer*'s Most Outstanding Wrestler for the fourth year in a row. Who was his 'pro' mentor when he competed on WWE's first season of the original NXT in 2010?

52. After which popular gimmick match was WWE's February 2010 pay-per-view named, becoming an annual event thereafter?

103

THE ULTIMATE WRESTLING QUIZ BOOK

53. In 2010, which WWE wrestler began offering grooming tips in the belief he was the most attractive superstar on the roster?

54. What three substances did CM Punk's Straight Edge Society abstain from?

55. How many years separated Bret Hart's No Holds Barred Lumberjack match with Vince McMahon at WrestleMania XXVI, and his previous appearance at WrestleMania?

56. Prior to making his main roster debut, Yoshi Tatsu competed in an FCW tag team called The Movers and The Shakers with which future WWE champion?

57. True or false? Every single men's match at WrestleMania XXVI, including the pre-show battle royal, featured a former or future WWE World Champion.

58. What was the name of the WWE internet show hosted by Cryme Tyme?

59. What was the name of the WWE-operated retail outlet in Toronto, Canada, which closed its doors in March 2011?

60. Which hardcore journeyman finally hung up his boots after 60 years in the industry in January 2011, at the age of 77?

THE PG ERA

61. NXT Season 3 contestant Lindsay 'Aloisia' Hayward was set to become WWE's tallest ever Diva, before the company nixed her appearance owing to her previous vocation as an erotic model. How tall was she?

62. What was the name of the one-time only pay-per-view WWE presented on the 20 June 2010, later used as the subheading of an NXT special?

63. Daniel Bryan was genuinely fired from WWE in June 2010 after choking announcer Justin Roberts too violently with what as part of a scripted angle on *Raw*?

64. How many of the original eight members of Wade Barrett's Nexus stable, a group of NXT contestants looking to displace WWE's old guard, went on to win world championships in the company in the next ten years?

65. What farmyard animal did Michelle McCool cruelly begin likening Mickie James to in December 2010, in mocking reference to her weight?

66. How many wrestlers competed in the bumper Royal Rumble 2011 match?

67. Which giant former WWE champion made a cameo in the above match, failing to eliminate anybody before being chucked out by Wade Barrett?

68. Who was the host of WrestleMania XXVII?

69. Jerry Lawler joined WWE in 1992, but he didn't wrestle a WrestleMania match until WrestleMania XXVII. Who was it against?

THE ULTIMATE WRESTLING QUIZ BOOK

70. Name the faction formed in January 2011 after splintering off from The Nexus.

71. What does 'Sin Cara' translate as?

72. True or false? Rey Mysterio became the shortest WWE Champion in the company's history when he won the belt on the 25 July 2011 episode of *Raw*.

73. What was unusual about Gail Kim's elimination from the Divas battle royal on the 1 August 2011 episode of *Raw*?

74. Which wrestler, the first to win NXT's Triple Crown, was squashed by Brodus Clay on the 29 September 2011 episode of *Superstars*?

75. True or false? Natalya Neidhart was the first woman to receive formal training in the Hart family 'Dungeon'.

76. In 2011, WWE presented the fifth season of NXT, subtitled '*Redemption*', in which rookies from previous seasons were given another shot at stardom. Which of the following ex-contestants did *not* participate?

    a) Derrick Bateman   b) Titus O'Neil
    c) Byron Saxton   d) Kaval

77. Whilst negotiating his WWE contract with Vince McMahon ahead of his clash with John Cena at Money in the Bank 2011, what confectionery item did CM Punk demand the company bring back?

THE PG ERA

78. Which US President was depicted on the poster for WWE's one-time only Washington, D.C. event Capitol Punishment, despite not appearing on the show?

79. For which independent promotion did CM Punk make an appearance in the week between his WWE contract 'expiring' at Money in the Bank 2011, and his return on the 25 June episode of *Raw*?

80. Who missed the Royal Rumble match for the first time in 14 years at Royal Rumble 2012?

81. True or false? Royal Rumble 2012 was Kharma's only match in WWE.

82. What was the tagline of WrestleMania XXVIII, headlined by John Cena vs. The Rock?

83. One year later, who main evented WrestleMania 29?

84. What character trait did WWE's Natalya develop in early 2012, much to the chagrin of critics and fans?

85. WrestleMania XXVIII was the most purchased wrestling event in history. Approximately how many people bought the show worldwide?

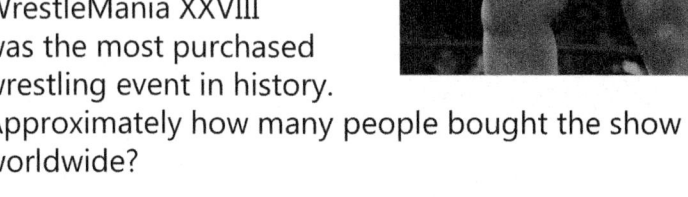

        a) 1.1 million **b)** 1.2 million
        c) 1.3 million **d)** 1.4 million

86. Which future AEW grappler did Ryback defeat, alongside enhancement talent Dan Delaney, as part of a handicap match at No Way Out 2012?

87. Amidst Linda McMahon's first candidacy attempt for the US Senate in 2010, her political opponents attempted to smear her campaign by raising WWE's previous ethical deficiencies. What was the name of the counter-initiative promoted by the company in an attempt to protect its image?

88. Which beloved festive figure did Alberto Del Rio accidentally mow down with his luxury car on the 24 December 2012 episode of *Raw*?

89. Matt Bloom returned to WWE from NJPW in 2012, where he adopted a new, Japanese-inspired persona known as 'Lord Tensai'. What was the name of his 'follower'?

90. Who made their WWE comeback at Extreme Rules 2012, eight years after quitting the company in 2004, only to lose to John Cena in the main event?

91. Brodus Clay's dancers Cameron and Naomi were collectively known as what?

92. True or false? Damien Sandow was the first man to fail to win a WWE World Championship after cashing in the Money in the Bank briefcase.

THE PG ERA

93. Jinder Mahal was portrayed as what relation to The Great Khali when he made his WWE debut?

94. In the office of which doctor did *Raw* GM AJ Lee compel Daniel Bryan and Kane to attend anger management classes, following their repeated fallings-out in 2012?

95. From which Floridian university did WWE begin running developmental meets in June 2012?

96. True or false? Following his WrestleMania 29 victory over Chris Jericho and subsequent *Raw* appearance, WWE ballroom dancer Fandango's theme music made it to #11 in the UK music charts.

97. What phrase from the United States Constitution was the catchphrase of the Real Americans?

98. In July 2013, WWE launched a reality show on E! Network known as what?

99. Which two championships were unified at TLC 2013?

100. Which long-running video-on-demand service shut down in January 2014 to make way for the WWE Network?

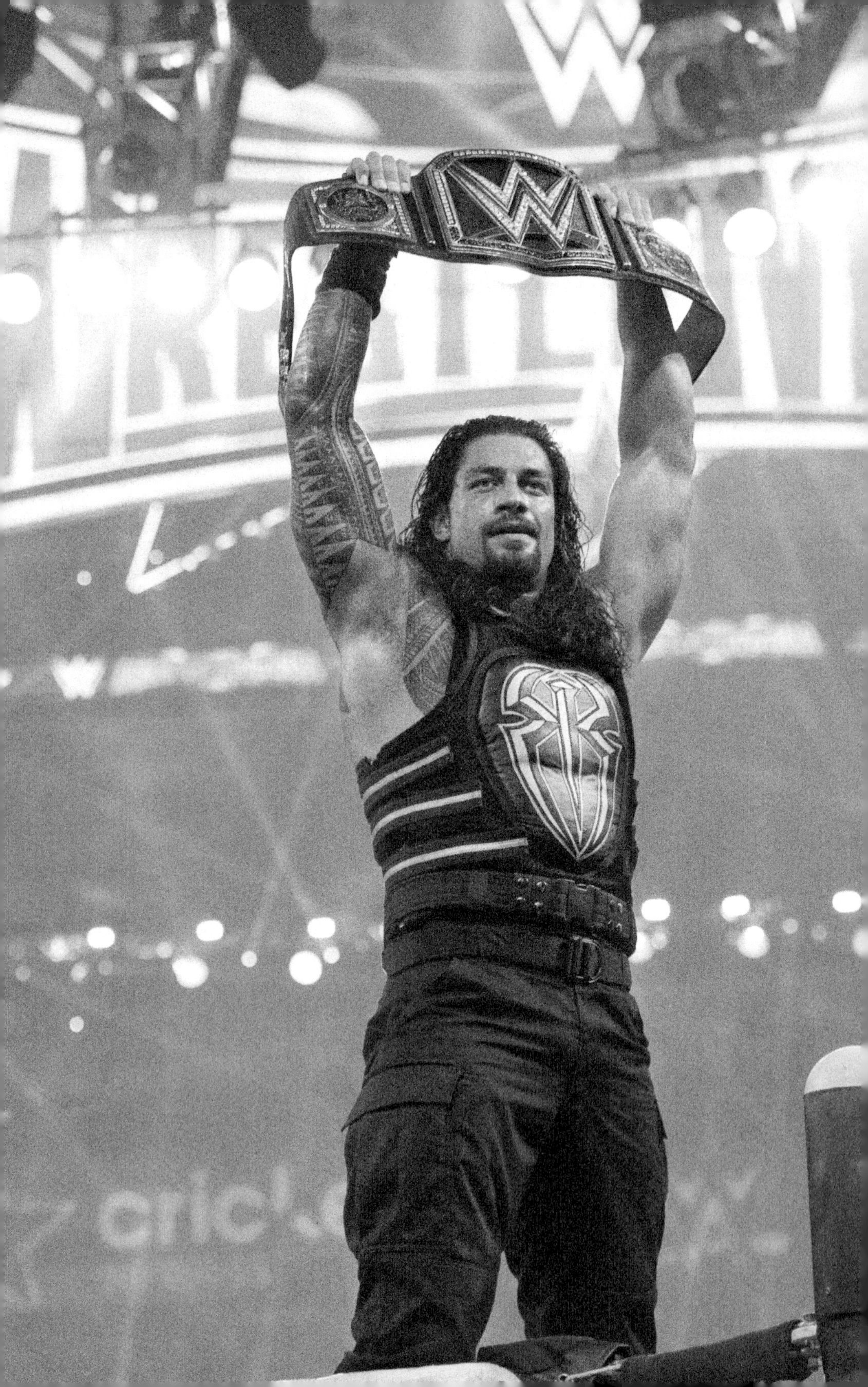

CHAPTER EIGHT

THE NETWORK

(Answers: P. 207)

1. From which backwoods cult did Daniel Bryan break free on the 13 January 2014, before defeating their leader at the Royal Rumble?

2. Who made their return to WWE in the number 28 slot at Royal Rumble 2014, after four years out of the company?

3. Which typically popular babyface received boos when he entered the above match at number 30, with the Pittsburgh crowd anticipating the arrival of Daniel Bryan?

4. The WWE Network officially launched on 24 February 2014. What was the first live wrestling match shown on the service?

5. What was the first NXT special to air on the WWE Network?

6. According to a disgruntled CM Punk, who walked out of WWE following Royal Rumble 2014, who was Daniel Bryan originally scheduled to face at WrestleMania XXX before the 'Yes! Movement' took hold?

7. Which stadium did WrestleMania XXX host Hulk Hogan inadvertently welcome fans to during his opening address on the show?

THE ULTIMATE WRESTLING QUIZ BOOK

8. From which Floridian ghost town were the Wyatt Family originally billed, before announcers ceased mentioning their hometown?

9. After succeeding in a WrestleMania XXX battle royal, Swiss superstar Cesaro won a trophy named after which WWE Hall of Famer?

10. The Undertaker's lengthy WrestleMania 'Streak' came to a close at the hands of Brock Lesnar at WrestleMania XXX, setting the score at 21-1. Who was the first wrestler to explicitly challenge Undertaker's record?

THE NETWORK

11. On 22 June 2014, Ring of Honor presented their first live pay-per-view, from Nashville's Tennessee State Fairground Sports Arena. What was it called?

12. Who did William Regal replace as General Manager of NXT in July 2014?

13. What was the call sign, spelled out in NATO's phonetic alphabet, heard at the start of The Shield's entrance music?

14. What was the main event of the first NXT TakeOver, held 29 May 2014?

15. True or false? Dave Bautista is an avid collector of vintage metal lunchboxes.

16. What does the term 'uso', adopted as the ringname of twins Jimmy and Jey, mean in their native Samoan?

17. Which of the following future WWE superstars did *not* previously appear as one of Adam Rose's entourage of 'Rosebuds'?

    a) Alexa Bliss   b) Kalisto
    c) Zelina Vega   d) Tyler Breeze

18. After disrespecting the nWo on the 19 January 2015 episode of *Raw*, The Ascension were cleared out by which two Attitude-era tag teams?

19. 'The Fifth Dimension' was the billed hometown of which face-painted WWE gimmick?

20. What was the name of the brief tag team formed by Summer Rae and Layla in June 2014?

THE ULTIMATE WRESTLING QUIZ BOOK

21. In which city was WWE's 'Ravishing Russian' Lana, born?

22. How many German suplexes did Brock Lesnar hit John Cena with during his destruction of the WWE Champion at SummerSlam 2014?

23. Sting's first WWE appearance in non-archival footage came during a WWE Network special chronicling the greatest matches of which superstar?

24. Who competed in a WWE match for the first time in 10 years at Royal Rumble 2015?

25. At WrestleMania 31, who became the first person born in the '90s to wrestle at the marquee event?

26. At NXT TakeOver: Fatal 4-Way, Pro Wrestling NOAH star KENTA was introduced to the brand as Hideo Itami. What does this name mean in English?

27. After a tag match between The Bella Twins and Paige & Emma ended in 29 seconds on the 23 February 2015 episode of *Raw*, what hashtag began trending on social media in support of WWE's underutilised female performers?

THE NETWORK

28. From what event in Irish history did Finn Bálor derive the name of his signature move, the 1916?

29. How many members of The Shield eventually became WWE 'Grand Slam' champions?

30. After being freed from the Wyatt Family in September 2015, Erick Rowan demonstrated his hitherto unknown genius by solving a Rubik's cube backstage. He was also said to be an expert in what agricultural process?

31. What event, held 28 April 2015, was the first non-NXT WWE show exclusive to the WWE Network?

32. At which prestigious Tokyo venue was WWE's 2015 Network special Beast in the East held?

33. What type of instrument was 'Francesa', which New Day member Xavier Woods could often be heard parping throughout his team's matches?

34. Charlotte Flair made her WWE main-roster debut on 13 July 2015. On which show did she make her first on-screen appearance in wrestling?

35. Which legendary Japanese junior heavyweight wrestled his one-and-only WWE match outside of Japan at NXT TakeOver: Brooklyn on 22 August 2015?

THE ULTIMATE WRESTLING QUIZ BOOK

36. What were Team PCB (a trio comprised of Becky Lynch, Charlotte Flair, and Paige) known as until WWE were alerted to the existence of a pornographic website of the same name?

37. True or false? Before entering pro-wrestling, Braun Strowman was a two-time winner of the Arnold Strongman Classic competition.

38. Who did Brock Lesnar defeat by disqualification in a United States title match on his only house show appearance of 2015?

39. In August 2015, NXT established an annual tag team tournament named in tribute of which former trainer and senior producer?

40. The 16 December 2015 NXT TakeOver was the first major show promoted by the brand in which country?

41. Newcastle-born NXT star Adrian Neville was named after which former Manchester United footballer and broadcaster?

42. Who was the only NXT wrestler to compete in the 2016 Royal Rumble match?

43. Which veteran Canadian actor narrated WWE Network series *Breaking Ground*, which followed the trials and tribulations of NXT hopefuls through their developmental training?

THE NETWORK

44. AJ Styles made a dramatic entrance at Royal Rumble 2016, entering the event in the number 3 slot. On which WWE C-show did he wrestle 14 years prior?

45. True or false? Brock Lesnar left Randy Orton needing stitches after SummerSlam 2016, after legitimately striking him in the head in an effort to draw blood.

46. In May 2016, WWE reintroduced the brand split that would see *Raw* and *SmackDown* assume separate rosters and championships. What other significant alteration occurred to *SmackDown*?

47. What was the record-breaking attendance claimed by WWE for WrestleMania 32, held at Arlington, TX's AT&T Stadium?

a) 80,355   b) 93,730   c) 98,645   d) 101,763

THE ULTIMATE WRESTLING QUIZ BOOK

48. In the autumn of 2016, Tenille 'Emma' Dashwood was given a storyline makeover and repackaged as what?

49. Which former WWE World Champion did Darren Young hire as his life coach in May 2016?

50. Just as Sami Zayn joined WWE, a masked indie star bearing a distinctly similar beard called El Generico coincidentally quit wrestling to do what?

51. The ring tights worn by Sasha Banks during her WrestleMania 32 triple threat match against Charlotte Flair and Becky Lynch were inspired by which WWE Hall of Famer?

52. In 2016, who became the first African-American woman inducted into WWE's Hall of Fame?

53. What was the name of the new Hall of Fame category WWE introduced in 2016, intended for stars of wrestling's early days?

54. True or false? During 2016 WWE promoted two pay-per-view events bearing the same name.

55. In August 2017, WWE held a 32-woman tournament known as the Mae Young Classic, named in honour of the WWE Hall of Famer. How many WWE championships did Young win throughout her lengthy career?

THE NETWORK

56. WWE's United Kingdom Championship tournament was held in which seaside resort?

57. Who commentated alongside Mauro Ranallo on WWE's 2016 32-man Cruiserweight Classic tournament?

58. Which of the following was *not* a participant in the above tournament?

    a) Kota Ibushi   **b)** Zack Sabre Jr.
    c) The Brian Kendrick   **d)** Ricochet

59. Which entertainment troupe did former NXT wrestler Mason Ryan join after quitting the industry in 2016?

60. At SummerSlam 2016, Finn Bálor became the inaugural WWE Universal Champion by defeating Seth Rollins. How many days did he hold the title for?

61. What was the weight limit for WWE's cruiserweight-centric Network exclusive show, which launched November 2016?

62. In 2014, Jeff and Karen Jarrett founded Global Force Wrestling. What was the name of the promotion's TV show, for which tapings were held in 2015, but not aired until 2017?

63. Why was the main event of No Mercy 2016, which pitted AJ Styles against Dean Ambrose and John Cena, moved to the start of the show?

THE ULTIMATE WRESTLING QUIZ BOOK

64. What forename links a contestant on WWE's 2004 Diva Search and the daughter of former WWE jobber Paul Van Dale, herself a WWE superstar?

65. What was the annual draft of talent to the *Raw* and *SmackDown* rosters rebranded as in April 2017?

66. At what apposite number did Tye Dillinger enter the 2017 Royal Rumble match?

67. Which of the following did Bray Wyatt *not* project onto the ring canvas during his WWE Championship match with Randy Orton at WrestleMania 33?

    a) Maggots b) Flies c) Worms d) Spiders

68. Who did Matt Hardy employ for landscaping services as part of his TNA 'Broken' Universe?

69. Who became the first women to main event a WWE pay-per-view at Hell in a Cell 2016?

70. Which gimmick match, invented by Dusty Rhodes, was revived for the NXT TakeOver held 18 November 2017?

71. After which philosophical principle were the members of NXT tag team The Authors of Pain named?

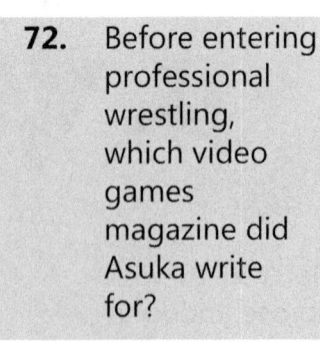

72. Before entering professional wrestling, which video games magazine did Asuka write for?

THE NETWORK

73. On which social media platform was WWE's Mixed Match Challenge originally aired?

74. How many pay-per-views/Network specials did WWE produce in 2017?

75. After which African capital city was Shinsuke Nakamura's trademark '*Bomaye*' finisher renamed in WWE?

76. How old was Tyler Bate when he became WWE's youngest singles champion in history by winning the United Kingdom Championship in 2017?

77. What did the '61' in Australian NXT tag-team TM-61 represent?

78. WWE's *Raw 25 Years*, which celebrated a quarter of a century of the Monday night show, was held at Brooklyn's Barclays Center and which Manhattan venue?

79. In March 2017, TNA rebranded under what name?

80. On the 5 April 2017 episode of *NXT*, Oney Lorcan defeated a masked musician known as 'El Vagabundo'. Who was beneath the mask?

THE ULTIMATE WRESTLING QUIZ BOOK

81. Who was revealed as Kurt Angle's illegitimate storyline son on the 17 July 2017 episode of *Raw*?

82. In September 2017, which day did Rusev proclaim as 'Rusev Day'?

83. The son of which WWE referee won WWE's *Raw* Tag Team Championship with Braun Strowman at WrestleMania 34, after the latter picked a fan out of the crowd to 'help' him beat The Bar?

84. Who recorded the most eliminations during the first ever women's Royal Rumble in 2018 - despite not being an active WWE superstar?

85. On the 13 February 2017 episode of *Raw*, Chris Jericho laid on a special ceremony for Kevin Owens called the Festival of Friendship, during which he presented his 'best friend' with a painting based on which world-famous Michelangelo fresco?

86. True or false? AJ Styles' victory over Jinder Mahal for the WWE Championship on the 7 November 2017 episode of *SmackDown* in Manchester, England, was the first time a WWE world championship had changed hands in Europe.

THE NETWORK

87. In June 2017, Netflix launched an Alison Brie-led series telling the story of which defunct women's wrestling league?

88. The name of which championship belt links Adam Cole and Ted DiBiase?

89. Linda McMahon finally accomplished her ambitions to enter the political sphere when US President Donald Trump appointed her in what role in 2017?

90. True or false? Charlotte Flair is the only woman to win any version of WWE's Women's Championship whose father also won one of the promotion's world titles.

91. Roman Reigns starred in the main event of WrestleMania for four consecutive years between WrestleMania 31 and WrestleMania 34. How many of his matches did he win?

92. True or False? Shinsuke Nakamura became the first wrestler born outside of North America to win the Royal Rumble when he triumphed in the 2018 edition.

THE ULTIMATE WRESTLING QUIZ BOOK

93. How many days did Asuka remain undefeated in WWE before eventually being beaten by Charlotte Flair at WrestleMania 34?

    a) 860 **b)** 914 **c)** 967 **d)** 1,002

94. WWE launched an annual Women's Battle Royal at WrestleMania 34. Which controversial wrestler was the match originally named for, before the company changed it due to fan backlash?

95. April 2018's Greatest Royal Rumble was the first show as part of WWE's partnership with which nation state?

96. A legitimate ex-sumo wrestler, never before seen in WWE, made an appearance in the above show's eponymous event, and was subsequently never heard from again. Who was it?

97. True or false? At 77:17, the Greatest Royal Rumble match became the longest match ever featured on a WWE pay-per-view.

98. Under what name did former WWE wrestler Enzo Amore release a rap album called *Rosemary's Baby Pt. 1: Happy Birthday* in November 2018?

99. In September 2018, independent supershow All In became the first non-WWE and non-WCW event to sell over 10,000 tickets in North America since which Mexican promotion managed the feat in 1994?

100. Cody vs. Nick Aldis at All In was contested for which historical wrestling championship?

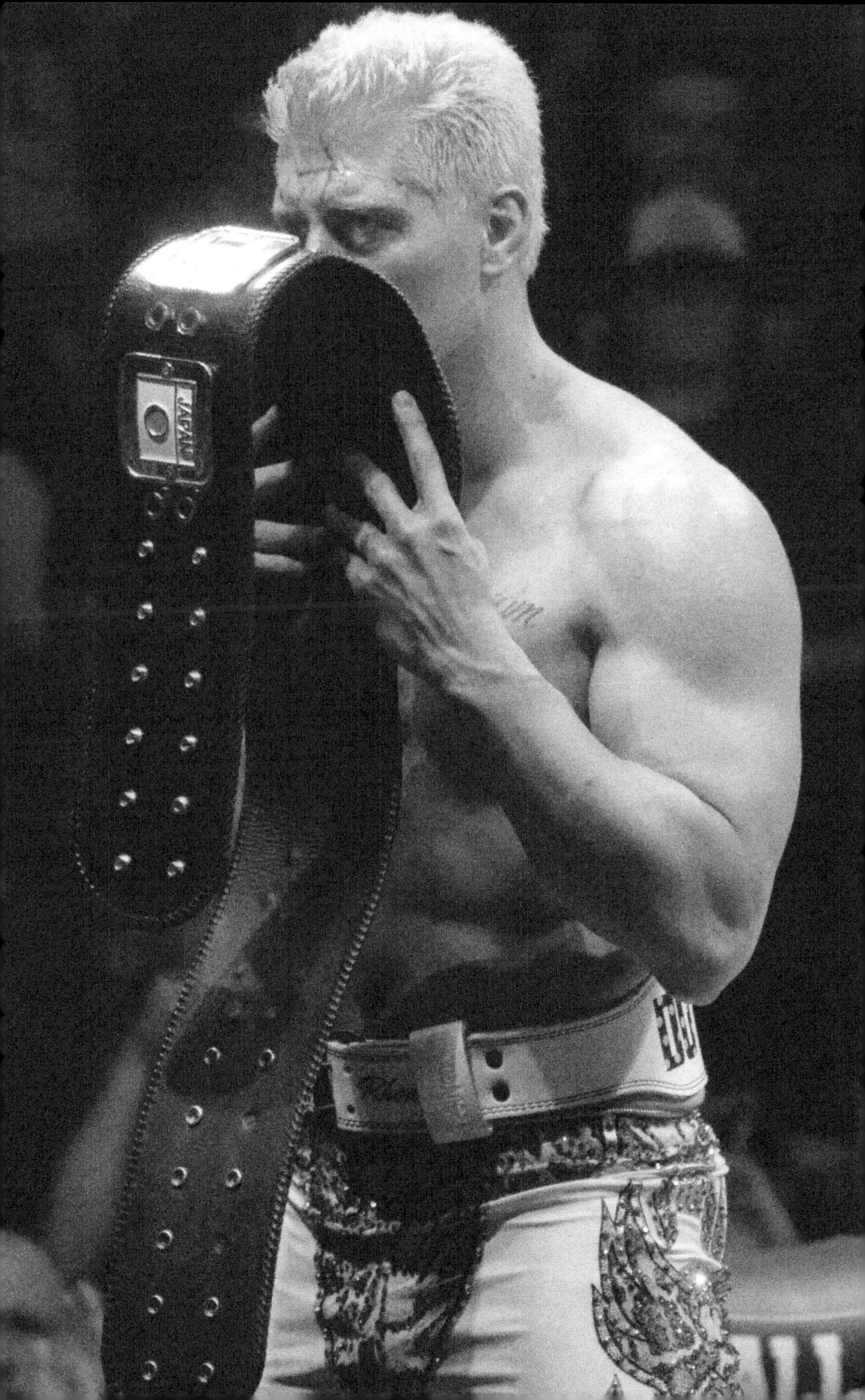

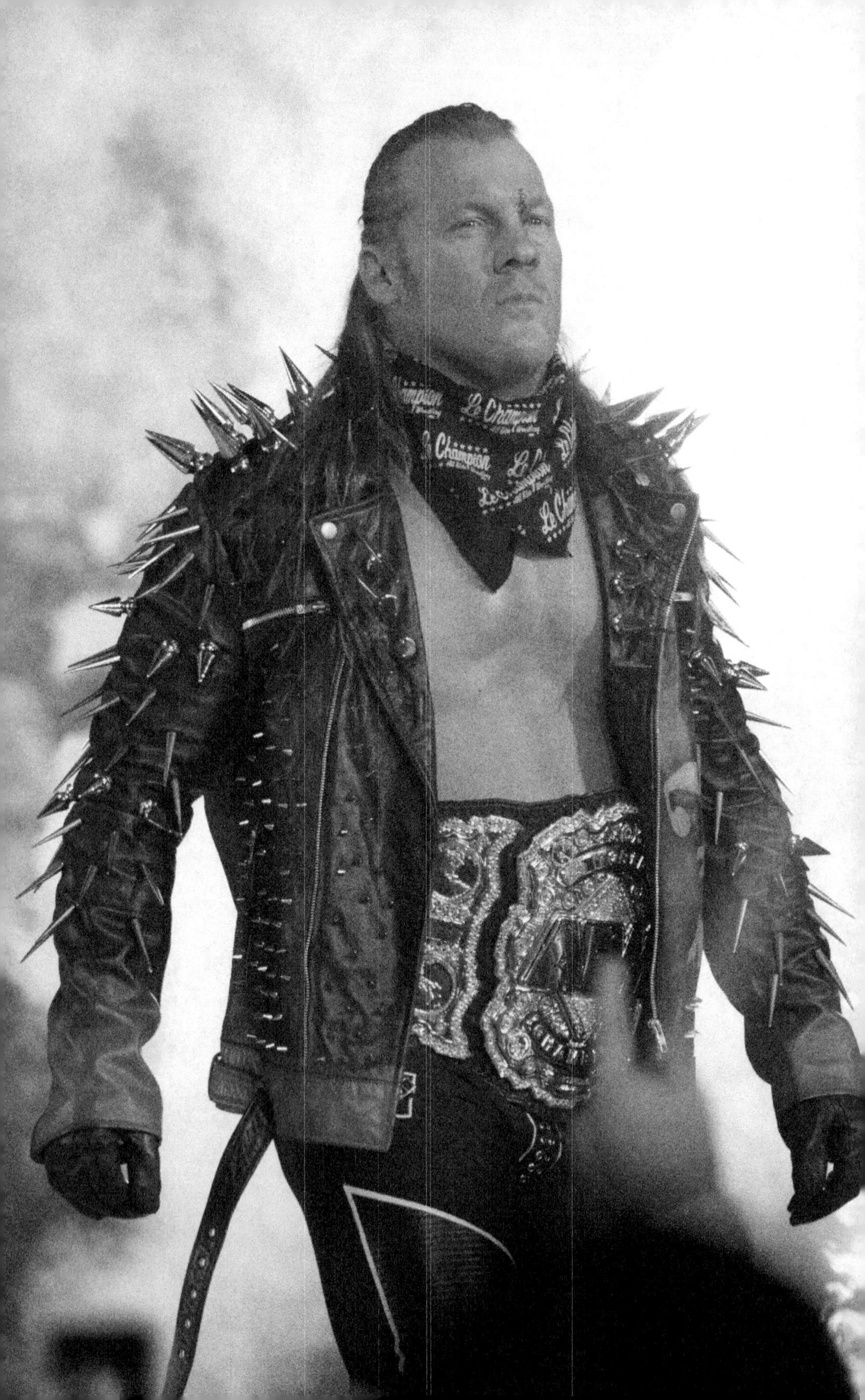
Le Champion

CHAPTER NINE

BEING ELITE

(Answers: P. 214)

1. In which country was the first WWE Super ShowDown, presented 6 October 2018, held?

2. True or false? WWE Evolution, held October 2018, was the first all-female North American wrestling pay-per-view.

3. What was the combined age of the four men who made up Crown Jewel 2018's main event?

4. Who gave Becky Lynch a legitimate concussion with a punch on the 12 November 2018 episode of *Raw*, resulting in her missing a Survivor Series match with Ronda Rousey?

5. Which team were announced as AEW's first roster signings at the company's January 2019 press rally?

6. True or false? Nyla Rose was announced on 2 January 2019 as AEW's first contracted female wrestler?

7. With which Chinese wrestling promotion did AEW announce a working relationship upon their formation?

8. How many women wrestled at Saudi Arabian show Crown Jewel, held just four days after WWE's progressive, all-female pay-per-view Evolution?

THE ULTIMATE WRESTLING QUIZ BOOK

9. What was the first singles match in AEW history, held during Double or Nothing 2019's 'Buy-In' pre-show?

10. How many wrestlers featured in Double or Nothing 2019's Casino Battle Royal had previously won championships in WWE?

11. Which multi-time wrestling Hall of Famer revealed the AEW World Championship belt during Double or Nothing 2019?

12. Over which championship did The Young Bucks and The Lucha Brothers compete at AEW Double or Nothing 2019?

13. What were Nordic-inspired tag team War Raiders known as during their first week on WWE's main roster, before their name was changed to Viking Raiders?

14. True or false? Nia Jax became the first wrestler to enter both a women's and men's Royal Rumble match when she participated in both at Royal Rumble 2019.

15. What prize was on offer for the winners of the 2018 WWE Mixed Match Challenge?

16. Name the wrestler: born Trevor Mann on 11 October 1988, he wrestled for PWG, Lucha Underground and NJPW before joining NXT in 2018.

BEING ELITE

17. True or false? Neither woman in the NXT UK Women's Championship match at the inaugural NXT UK TakeOver was from the United Kingdom.

18. Kairi Sane's 'Sky Pirate' gimmick was inspired by her pre-wrestling background in what competitive sport?

19. What was the name of the NXT, NXT UK, and 205 Live branded WWE Network special held across 26 and 27 January 2019?

20. On the 29 January 2019 episode of *SmackDown*, WWE Champion and vegan Daniel Bryan replaced his leather title belt with a new version made of what?

21. What was the name of the WWE special event aired during the SuperBowl in 1999 and once more in 2019?

22. Who was advertised in Elimination Chamber 2019's eponymous match for the WWE Championship, only to pull out through injury?

23. The name of AEW's second major show, held 29 June 2019 in Daytona Beach, FL, was a parody of which fraudulent festival?

24. AEW's Fight for the Fallen was a charity event with the proceeds contributing to victims of what?

25. Which Saturday Night Live writer and comedian did Braun Strowman eliminate last to win WrestleMania 35's Andre the Giant Memorial Battle Royal?

26. How many consecutive defeats had Curt Hawkins suffered when he finally broke his losing run at WrestleMania 35?

27. Which hit did rock 'n' roll veteran Joan Jett perform live for Ronda Rousey's entrance at WrestleMania 35?

28. WrestleMania 35 was the third WrestleMania The Undertaker had missed since his debut at the event in 1991. Name the other two he was absent from.

29. Which two women travelled to Jeddah, Saudi Arabia for a match at WWE's Super ShowDown 2019, only for the plan to be rejected by the Saudi government?

30. In November 2019, former Wyatt Family member Rowan began carrying a cage of which the contents were concealed by a cloth. What was eventually revealed to be in the cage?

31. Who did Matt Riddle describe as "the worst wrestler in the business [...] unsafe, dangerous, and a liability to everyone else" following a disastrous match at WWE Super ShowDown 2019?

32. True or false? WWE's 'Classy Southern Belle' Lacey Evans served in the US Marines' Special Reaction Team before embarking on a professional wrestling career.

BEING ELITE

33. What was the name of the one-time only WWE pay-per-view held 23 June 2019, main evented by Seth Rollins vs. Baron Corbin?

34. The 10th anniversary of which independent wrestling outfit was aired on the WWE Network on 13 July 2019?

35. Name the second-generation wrestler, who made a single AEW appearance as part of All Out 2019's Casino Battle Royal.

36. The brief alliance of The Undertaker and Roman Reigns, which took on Shane McMahon and Drew McIntyre at Extreme Rules 2019, was informally known as what?

THE ULTIMATE WRESTLING QUIZ BOOK

37. Name the July 2019 WWE Network special from Nashville, TN, which featured a musical concert by songster Elias.

38. On which reality TV show was Austin Matelson (better known as AEW's prehistoric reptile Luchasaurus) a contestant in 2015?

39. In April 2019, Bray Wyatt began hosting a surreal parody of a children's television show called the 'Firefly Fun House'. After which former WWE superstar was the buzzard puppet on the satirical skit named?

40. Who defeated Hangman Page to become the inaugural AEW World Champion at All Out?

41. True or false? In 2019, Bayley became the first woman in WWE to win the clean sweep of women's *Raw*, *SmackDown*, NXT and Tag Team championships.

42. What was unusual about the way the Hell in a Cell match between Seth Rollins and The Fiend ended at WWE Hell in a Cell 2019?

43. The tag team of Asuka and Kairi Sane were named after which form of classical Japanese theatre?

BEING ELITE

44. The debut episode of AEW *Dynamite*, aired 2 October 2019, became the first wrestling show since 26 March 2001 to be broadcast on which television network?

45. Which English comedian, best known for co-writing BBC sitcom The Office, directed a 2019 biopic based on the career of Paige?

46. What did Brandi Rhodes and Awesome Kong snatch from their beaten opponents as a trophy during their time in short-lived AEW stable The Nightmare Collective?

47. True or false? AEW's Dynamite Diamond Ring, first won outright by MJF in November 2019, is worth $100,000.

48. True or false? Despite being billed as Shorty G on account of his height in 2019, Olympian and amateur wrestling star Chad Gable was actually taller than the American male average.

49. Two teams of five men represented which two WWE Hall of Famers in a 10-man tag team match at Crown Jewel 2019?

50. At Crown Jewel 2019, Braun Strowman lost via countout to which British boxing star?

51. Which WWE brand emerged victorious at the end of Survivor Series 2019, having won four of the seven inter-brand matches?

THE ULTIMATE WRESTLING QUIZ BOOK

52. True or false? Asuka and Kairi Sane became the first Asian-born wrestlers to main event a WWE pay-per-view, when they faced Becky Lynch and Charlotte Flair at TLC 2019?

53. Who became the first man to win both WWE's original Hardcore championship and its 2019 equivalent, the 24/7 Championship, when he pinned an unsuspecting Drake Maverick on the 22 July 2019 edition of *Raw*?

54. True or false? Dr. Britt Baker D.M.D. holds a real life qualification in dentistry.

55. Following its move to USA Network on Wednesdays in October 2019, on how many occasions did NXT beat AEW in the Wednesday night ratings battle before switching to Tuesdays in April 2021?

56. What is the name of AEW's training facility, operated by wrestler QT Marshall?

57. Cody Rhodes' defeat to Chris Jericho at Full Gear 2019 stipulated that he would never be able to do what in AEW again?

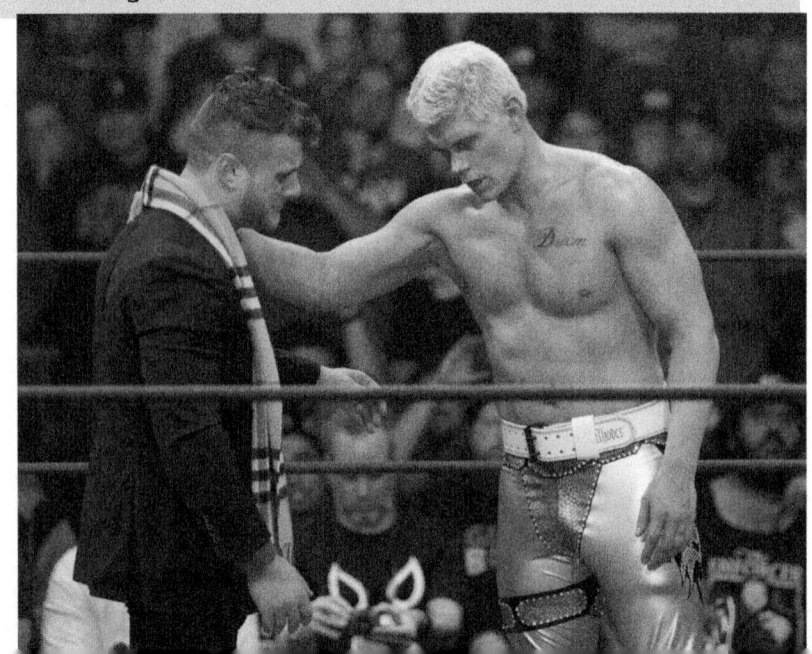

BEING ELITE

58. Who made history by becoming the first woman to hold the Impact World Championship, when she defeated Sami Callihan for the title at 12 January 2021's Hard to Kill?

59. At Royal Rumble 2020, Brock Lesnar equalled Braun Strowman's record for most eliminations in a single match. How many did he rack up?

60. Who made an emotional WWE return during the 2020 men's Royal Rumble match, nine years after a neck injury had forced him to retire?

61. On which cruise ship did Chris Jericho's *Rock 'N' Wrestling Rager at Sea Part Deux: Second Wave*, an event combining wrestling and rock and roll, take place?

62. What trophy did The Undertaker win at Super ShowDown 2020, after overcoming AJ Styles at the conclusion of a six-man gauntlet match?

63. What AEW Revolution 2020 tag team match did *Wrestling Observer*'s Dave Meltzer review as "the greatest tag team match in wrestling history"?

THE ULTIMATE WRESTLING QUIZ BOOK

64. What was the official combined attendance for WrestleMania 36?

65. True or false? With matches filmed in Orlando, FL and Stamford, CT, WrestleMania 36 became the first WrestleMania to be held in two different cities.

66. Supposed alien Kris Statlander is billed from which galaxy?

67. Where were the simultaneous men and women's Money in the Bank ladder matches held at WWE Money in the Bank 2020?

68. Which historical pay-per-view series did WWE revive for 7 June 2020's NXT TakeOver?

69. The main event match between Edge and Randy Orton at Backlash 2020 was billed as what?

70. In what sort of cinematic match did Bray Wyatt defeat Braun Strowman at WWE's spooky-themed 2020 event, The Horror Show at Extreme Rules?

71. Due to the 2020 COVID-19 pandemic, WWE were forced to play before empty arenas. What was the name of the bio-secure video-conference system the company introduced in August 2020 as a way of allowing fans to virtually appear at ringside?

72. What was the similar set-up introduced to NXT called, named in homage of WWE's pre-cursor operation?

BEING ELITE

73. Roman Reigns returned to WWE from sabbatical at SummerSlam 2020, after which he adopted a new 'Tribal Chief' character. As part of the gimmick, he started wearing a traditional Samoan necklace known as an *ula fala*. What colour was it?

74. Orange Cassidy defeated Chris Jericho at AEW All Out 2020 by submerging him into a vat of what cocktail?

75. AEW Double or Nothing's novel 'Stadium Stampede' match took place within the stadium of which NFL team?

76. Which of the following was *not* a member of WWE's stable of disgruntled superstars known as Retribution?

    a) T-Bar b) Mace c) Reckoning d) Blackjack

77. True or false? The Undertaker wrestled a 'retirement match' at Survivor Series, as the show celebrated his 30th year in the company.

78. From which video game did Kenny Omega derive the name of his finisher, the One Winged Angel?

137

79. What brutal (storyline) fate befell The Fiend at the conclusion of his 'Firefly Inferno' match with Randy Orton at WWE TLC 2020?

80. WWE's Superstar Spectacle was a one-off WWE Network special designed to coincide with which country's 'Republic Day' (the date on which its constitution came into effect)?

81. Edge lasted 58:30 to win the 2021 men's Royal Rumble, having entered the contest in the number 1 position. How many opponents did he eliminate whilst going coast-to-coast?

82. How old was Sting when he made his competitive AEW debut at Revolution 2021, in a cinematic street fight alongside Darby Allin against Brian Cage and Ricky Starks?

83. What happened for the first time in WrestleMania history at WrestleMania 37, resulting in a 30 minute pause in proceedings?

84. Which Puerto Rican recording artist teamed with Damian Priest to defeat The Miz & John Morrison at WrestleMania 37?

85. 2021's edition of regular WWE pay-per-view Backlash was prefixed with the name of which other event?

86. True or false? 2021 was the first year in which three wrestlers successfully cashed in Money in the Bank contracts.

BEING ELITE

87. In March 2021, AEW launched a third weekly programme with a focus on emerging talent called what?

88. Who won the 21 man Casino Battle Royal at AEW Double or Nothing 2021?

89. True or false? CM Punk's AEW debut on the first episode of the company's new show, Rampage, was his first appearance at a wrestling event since departing WWE in 2014.

90. Which NJPW veteran did Jon Moxley defeat at AEW All Out 2021?

91. 2021's SummerSlam was the first to be held in a stadium since when?

92. An AEW TNT special held 2 December 2020 was named for a phrase from which popular fantasy television series?

93. In March 2021, the WWE Network was folded into which NBC-operated streaming service?

94. At Crown Jewel 2021, Zelina Vega became the first woman to win the Queen's Crown tournament, a newly minted female equivalent of the long-running King of the Ring contest. Who was the first woman to use the title 'Queen' in WWE?

95. What number did Anna Jay adopt when joining AEW cult The Dark Order?

96. 'Grand Slam', AEW's 22 September 2021 special, was held at which famous New York tennis venue?

97. Which long-running independent promotion released all its talent from their contracts in December 2021, and announced they would be going on hiatus?

98. What artefact did WWE Chairman Vince McMahon arrive at Survivor Series 2021 holding, having been gifted it by The Rock?

99. Who performed under a mask as 'Infinito' on the 30 November episode of AEW Dark?

100. In August 2021, WWE announced Day 1, the first annual pay-per-view in the company's history to take place on which date?

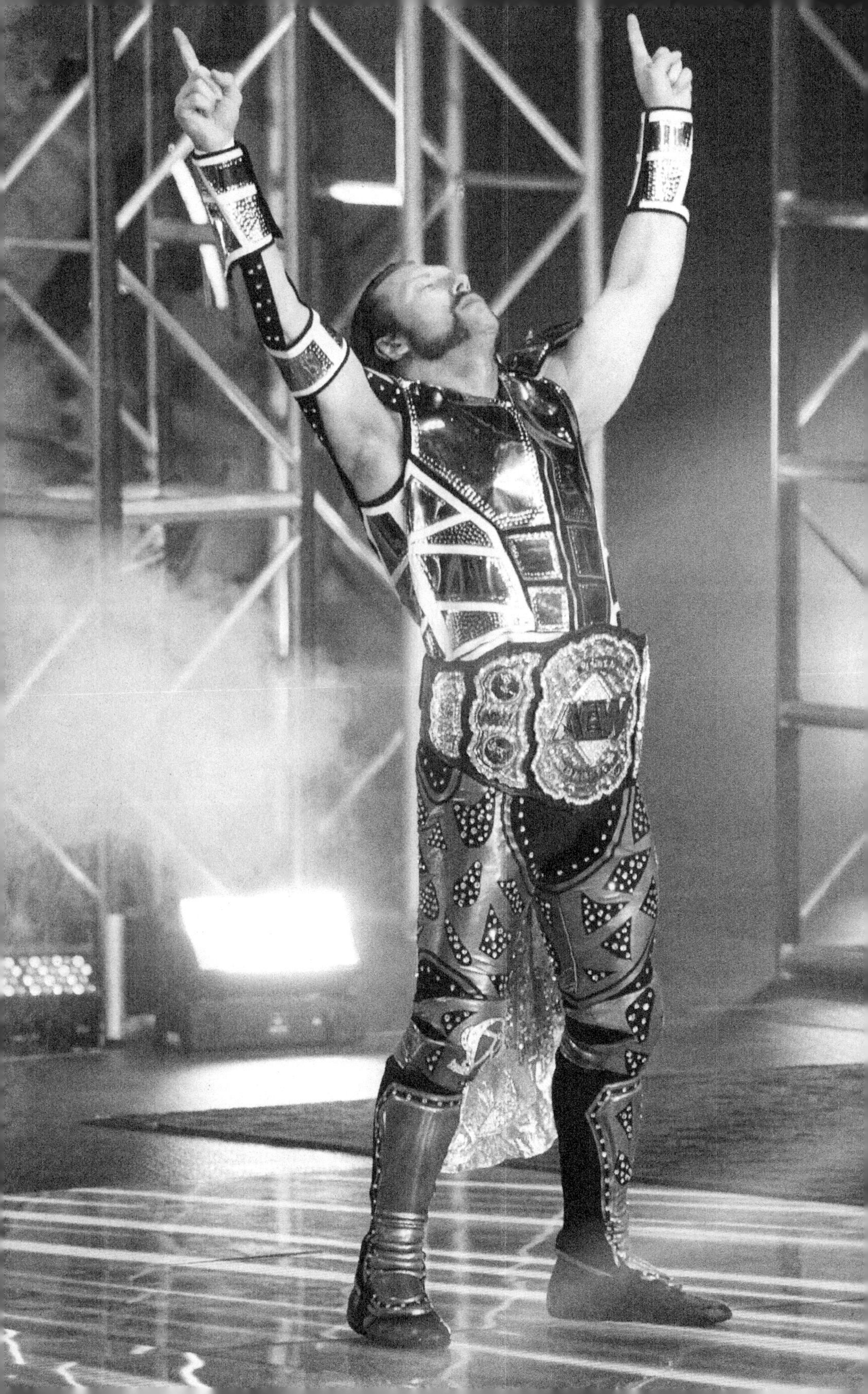
AEW

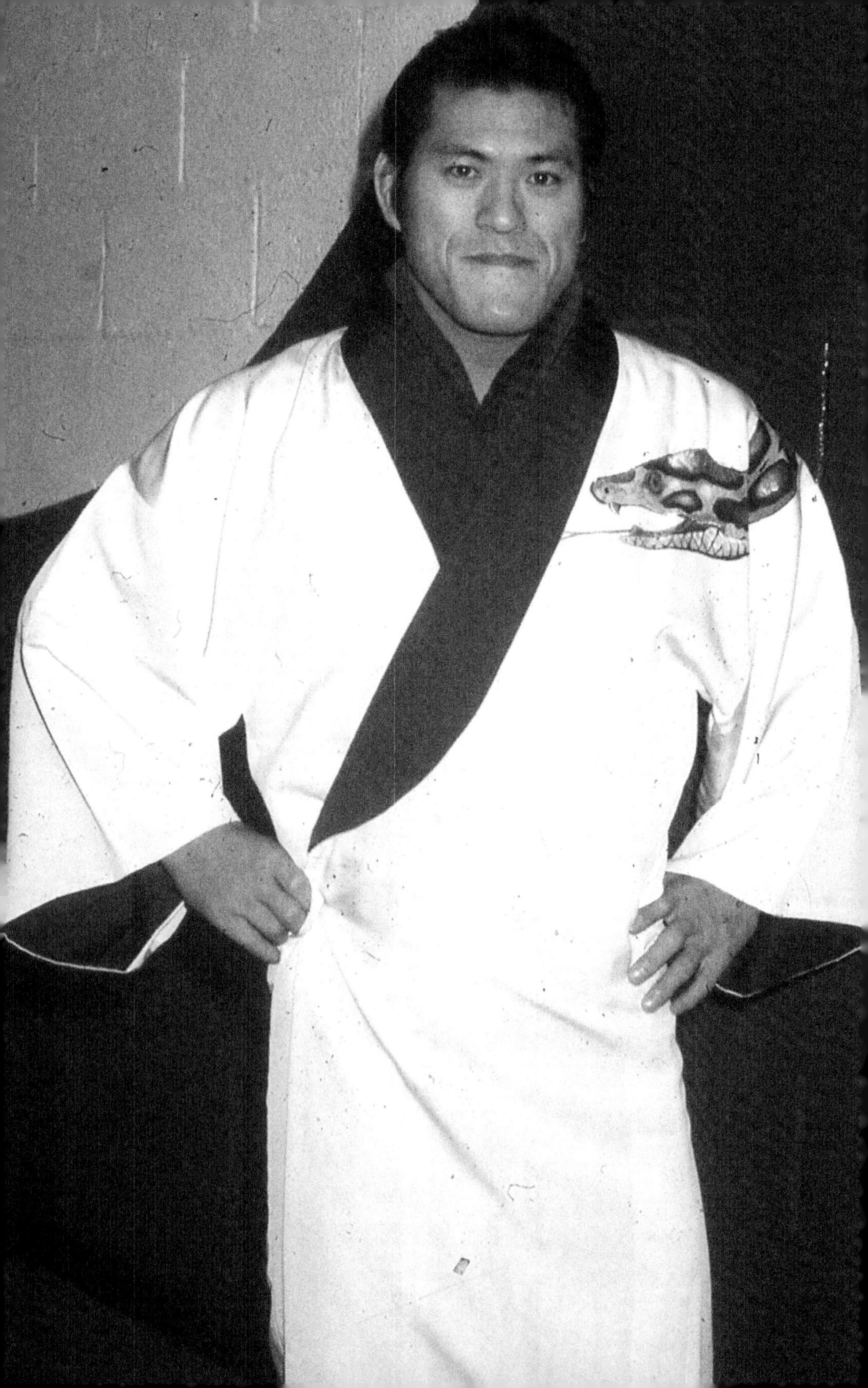

CHAPTER TEN

PURORESU

(Answers: P. 220)

1. Which Korea-born Japanese wrestling icon became known as the 'Father of Puroresu'?

2. What was the name of Japan's first professional wrestling promotion, established in 1953?

3. Following his departure from the above company, who founded New Japan Pro Wrestling in 1972, ?

4. Toshiyuki 'Harold' Sakata, a one-time All Asia Tag Team Champion alongside Rikidozan, starred in a James Bond film as which villainous henchman?

5. What is the slogan of NJPW, as seen on the outfit's logo?

6. Who was the first man to defend an NWA-sanctioned championship in Japan?

7. Name the Japanese promotion, which operated between 1966 and 1981, that held the first ever cage match in the country.

8. What is the name of the governing body founded by NJPW which oversees the company's championships?

9. Name the wrestling promotion founded October 1972 by Shohei 'Giant' Baba, and Rikidozan's sons, Mitsuo and Yoshihiro Momota.

10. What was the billed height of Japanese wrestling icon Shohei 'Giant' Baba?

a) 6'5" **b)** 6'8"
c) 6'10" **d)** 7'0"

11. Name the wrestler: the trainer of Hulk Hogan and Lex Luger, his ring name was derived from Sorakichi Matsuda, Japan's first professional wrestler.

12. Ahead of their exhibition 'boxing vs. wrestling' fight in June 1976, what type of bird did Muhammad Ali refer to Antonio Inoki as on account of his prominent chin?

13. Expecting Inoki to easily out-wrestle - and embarrass - his opponent in the above fight, Muhammad Ali's camp insisted on a number of rules, including that Inoki could not kick Ali unless one knee was on the mat. As a consequence, how many times did Inoki, on his back, kick Ali in the shins during the match?

a) 55 **b)** 78 **c)** 107 **d)** 156

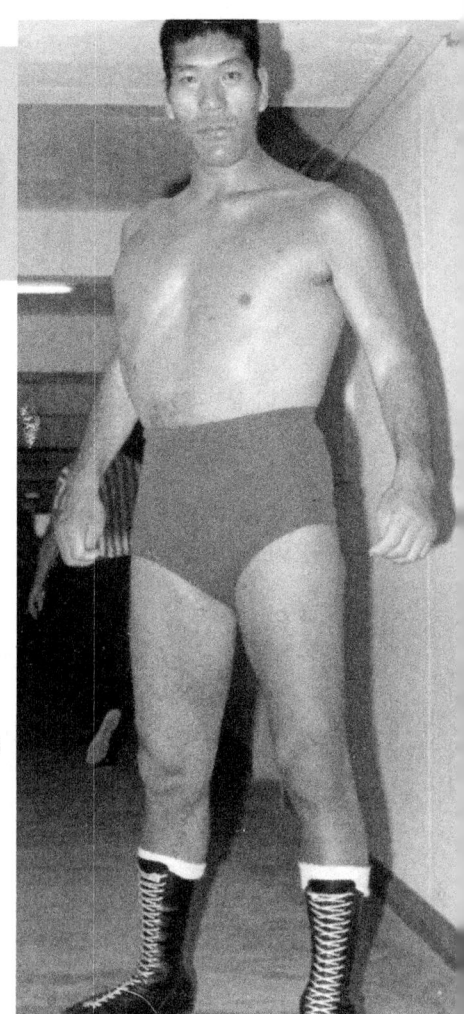

PURORESU

14. What was the name of the championship awarded to Antonio Inoki by Vince McMahon in December 1978, which he went on to hold for a combined total of 4,000 days across two reigns?

15. Which Canadian was the first non-Japanese wrestler to win AJPW's annual Champion Carnival tournament?

16. True or false? Hulk Hogan was the first holder of the original IWGP Heavyweight Championship.

17. In 1983, Satoru 'Tiger Mask' Sayama suddenly quit professional wrestling, having grown jaded with its 'fake' nature. What was the name of the tell-all book about the industry he released shortly afterwards?

18. What was the name of the mixed martial arts outfit Sayama started in 1986?

19. Whilst working as the second iteration of Tiger Mask, what move did Mitsuharu Misawa innovate in order to beat Kuniaki Kobayashi for the NWA International Junior Heavyweight Championship on 31 August 1985?

20. The winner of a new version of the IWGP Heavyweight Championship was crowned at the climax of NJPW's 1987 International Wrestling Grand Prix. Which future WWF Intercontinental Champion competed in the tournament?

THE ULTIMATE WRESTLING QUIZ BOOK

21. 'Victory through Guts' was the slogan of which *joshi* wrestling promotion?

22. Chigusa Nagoyo and Lioness Asuka were collectively known as what?

23. How many of the first three IWGP Heavyweight Champions lost the title in the ring?

24. Battle Satellite, held 24 April 1989, was the first show NJPW held at which Tokyo venue?

25. Who became the first European to win the IWGP Heavyweight Championship by defeating Big Van Vader on 25 May 1989?

26. The trio of Keiji Mutoh, Masahiro Chono and Shinya Hashimoto, each a graduate of the NJPW Dojo, were collectively known as what?

27. The name of which AJPW star was decided by a fan contest, as the company considered his given name, Tomomi, to be too feminine?

PURORESU

28. What is the name of AJPW's highest honour, established 18 April 1989 following the unification of the PWF World Heavyweight, NWA United National, and NWA International Heavyweight championships?

29. What acronym links promotions ran by Hisashi Shinma, Bill Watts, and Herb Abrams?

30. What was the name of the 13 April 1990 supershow jointly promoted by NJPW/AJPW and WWF?

31. In April 1990, Genichiro Tenryu left AJPW to become a spokesmodel for Megane Super, who in turn launched a multi-million yen wrestling outfit. What product was Megane Super a leading manufacturer of in Japan?

32. What was the name of the promotion they subsequently formed, whose motto was 'Straight and Strong'?

33. And what was the original full name of the above federation's successor, abbreviated to WAR?

34. On what date is NJPW's Tokyo Dome show traditionally held?

35. With which American wrestling company did NJPW co-produce the first of these shows in 1992?

36. Who teamed with The Great Muta to defeat the Steiner Bros. in the main event of the above show?

37. What was the name of NJPW's first hall of fame, established in 1990 to celebrate the 30th year of Antonio Inoki's career?

38. Who comprised the celebrated early '90s AJPW quartet informally known as the 'Four Pillars of Heaven'?

39. Minoru Suzuki was amongst the founding members of which hybrid MMA/wrestling promotion, named for a Greek sport at the Ancient Olympic Games?

40. True or false? Before the outbreak of the Gulf War, Antonio Inoki held successful negotiations with Iraqi dictator Saddam Hussein over the release of Japanese hostages.

41. What term describes the long-term narrative style of booking promoted by AJPW's Giant Baba throughout the '90s?

42. Japanese hardcore wrestling innovator and founder of Frontier Martial-Arts Wrestling, Atsushi Onita, was known as 'Namida no Karisuma'. What does this mean in English?

43. True or false? FMW once promoted a No Rope Electrified Barbed Wire Swimming Pool Dynamite Double Hell Death Match.

PURORESU

44. Who won the first NJPW Best of the Super Juniors tournament in 1994?

45. What had the tournament previously been known as between 1988 and 1994?

46. Name the wrestler: born Eiji Ezajki on 29 November 1968, he starred for FMW and was notably featured on ECW's Heat Wave '98 pay-per-view, tagging with Jinsei Shinzaki against RVD & Sabu.

47. Veteran Japanese wrestling referee Hiroyuki Umino is better known as what, on account of his notable footwear?

48. Named for a violent 14 September 1990 encounter between The Great Muta and Hiroshi Hase, what factor does the 'Muta scale' measure?

49. What is the name of Jushin Liger's violent alter-ego, first seen after The Great Muta attempted to unmask the junior heavyweight in 1996?

50. How many concurrent championships did Ultimo Dragon hold between 29 December 1996 and 4 January 1997?

51. The Antonio Inoki Retirement Show, held 4 April 1998, holds the record attendance for any Japanese wrestling event. 70,000 people packed into the Tokyo Dome to see a show headlined by what match?

THE ULTIMATE WRESTLING QUIZ BOOK

52. Which of the following was *not* a gimmick match used by deathmatch specialists Big Japan Pro Wrestling?

    a) Crocodile Deathmatch   **c)** Scorpion Deathmatch
    b) Piranha Deathmatch   **d)** Shark Deathmatch

53. What was the objective of FMW's crude 1999 gimmick contest known as the 'Anus Explosion Death Match'?

54. In response to MMA's growing popularity in Japan, NJPW introduced shoot elements to its matches in the early 2000s. What did this style of wrestling become known as, after its chief proponent?

55. Name the wrestler: born Erika Shishido on 25 September 1970, she set up a promotion called Hyper Visual Fighting Arsion after working for JWA for over a decade.

56. Name the woman who became majority owner of AJPW following the death of her husband in January 1999.

57. After which Biblical figure did Mitsuharu Misawa name a breakaway wrestling organisation, formed June 2000, following his exit from AJPW?

PURORESU

58. What is the name of that company's highest championship, established 15 April 2001?

59. After returning from excursion in 2001, Keiji Mutoh formed a stable alongside Shinjiro Otani and Don Frye. What was it called?

60. Which former three-time WWE Tag Team Champion lost in the final of AJPW's 2002 Champion Carnival to Keiji Mutoh?

61. In 2005, who became only the second man to win NJPW's G1 Climax five times, after Antonio Inoki?

62. Throughout his career, how many of Mitsuharu Misawa's matches received a five star or higher rating from *Wrestling Observer*'s Dave Meltzer?

   a) 15   b) 20
   c) 25   d) 30

63. In 2007, Antonio Inoki left NJPW to form his own MMA/wrestling hybrid promotion. What was it called?

64. Which two former WWE champions headlined the outfit's first show?

THE ULTIMATE WRESTLING QUIZ BOOK

65. In 1997, four wrestlers from Pro Wrestling Crusaders founded their own promotion, known as Dramatic Dream Team Pro-wrestling. What is the name of the company's largest annual show, first held 1999?

66. From which video game did NJPW and AJPW's joint 35th anniversary show in 2007 derive its name?

67. The main event of the above show was booked in tribute to which wrestler, who died of a cerebral haemorrhage in 2005?

68. During his spell in NJPW, what did Brock Lesnar rename his F-5 finisher owing to an ongoing lawsuit with WWE?

69. In 2007, the king of deathmatches Atsushi Onita released a video game quiz for the Nintendo DS on what subject?

70. What is the name of the NJPW stable formed by Toru Yano and Shinsuke Nakamura?

71. In 2010, NJPW devised NEVER, a series of events designed to showcase emerging talent. What did the 'V' in the acronym stand for?

72. In which state was the first show of NJPW's 2011 tour of the USA held, their first ever in the country?

PURORESU

73. After forming the Time Splitters tag team with Alex Shelley, KUSHIDA began wearing attire inspired by which iconic '80s movie character?

74. Rookies graduating from NJPW's dojos are known within the company as what?

75. True or false? Kenta Kobashi's 'Burning Hammer' finisher (an inverted Death Valley Driver), was so dangerous that he only used it 14 times throughout his career?

76. In which city is NJPW's annual Dominion event traditionally held?

77. Bad Intentions, who set a record 564 day reign with the IWGP Tag Team Championship between 2010 and 2012, was made up of which two American wrestlers?

78. Name the top championship associated with Dragon Gate, established June 2004.

79. What was the name of Kenta Kobashi's retirement show, hosted by Pro Wrestling NOAH on 11 May 2013?

80. Who won the IWGP Heavyweight Championship for a 5th time at Wrestle Kingdom V, kick-starting a record setting 404 day reign the belt?

81. The NJPW team consisting of Beretta and Rocky Romero were named for which prosperous Tokyo district?

82. Which of the following did *not* gain a seat in the Japanese Diet (the country's parliament) following their wrestling career?

   a) Tatsumi Fujinami **b)** Hiroshi Hase
   c) Antonio Inoki   **d)** Atsushi Onita

83. In 2013, Prince Devitt formed an all-foreign stable known as The Bullet Club with Karl Anderson, Tama Tonga, and which other wrestler?

84. What was the name of New Japan Super Junior Hiromu Takahashi's pet 'cat' (actually a stuffed toy)?

85. Which future multi-time IWGP Heavyweight Champion had a brief run in TNA wearing a bandit's mask under the name Okato?

86. Which of the following has *not* won DDT's parody Ironman Heavymetalweight Championship?

   a) A ladder   **b)** A trash can
   c) A monkey   **d)** The championship belt itself

87. Hiroshi Tanahashi faced Shinsuke Nakamura in the main event of Wrestle Kingdom 8 for which championship?

PURORESU

88. Who succeeded Prince Devitt as leader of the Japanese Bullet Club following his departure from NJPW in 2014?

89. Who became the sixth incarnation of Tiger Mask, known as Tiger Mask W, in conjunction with an anime series of the same name in 2016?

90. The NJPW tag team comprised of Kenny Omega and Kota Ibushi were collectively known as what?

91. What was unusual about DDT wrestler YOSHIHIKO?

92. What is the catchphrase associated with Los Ingobernables de Japón founder Tetsuya Naito?

93. Chris Jericho's 2018 confrontation with Kenny Omega at Wrestle Kingdom 12 was his first NJPW match in 20 years. What was the name of the gimmick - the nemesis of Jushin Liger - which he portrayed on his debut for the company in January 1997?

94. True or false? Kazuchika Okada vs. Kenny Omega at Wrestle Kingdom 11 was the first match in history to be awarded a six star rating by *Wrestling Observer*'s Dave Meltzer.

155

THE ULTIMATE WRESTLING QUIZ BOOK

95. 'Artist', 'Goddess', and 'High Speed' are all names of championships in which Japanese wrestling federation?

96. What is the name of NJPW's online streaming service, launched 1 December 2014?

97. Who became NJPW's first IWGP United States Heavyweight Champion after beating Tomohiro Ishii in a tournament final at the G1 Special in USA on 2 July 2017?

98. In 1989, Human Entertainment released the first in a long-running Japanese wrestling video game series known as what?

99. What is the only Japanese wrestling championship which was held by Rikidozan, Giant Baba, and Antonio Inoki?

100. At which historic New York venue was NJPW's Wrestle Dynasty event scheduled to take place, only to be cancelled owing to the COVID-19 pandemic?

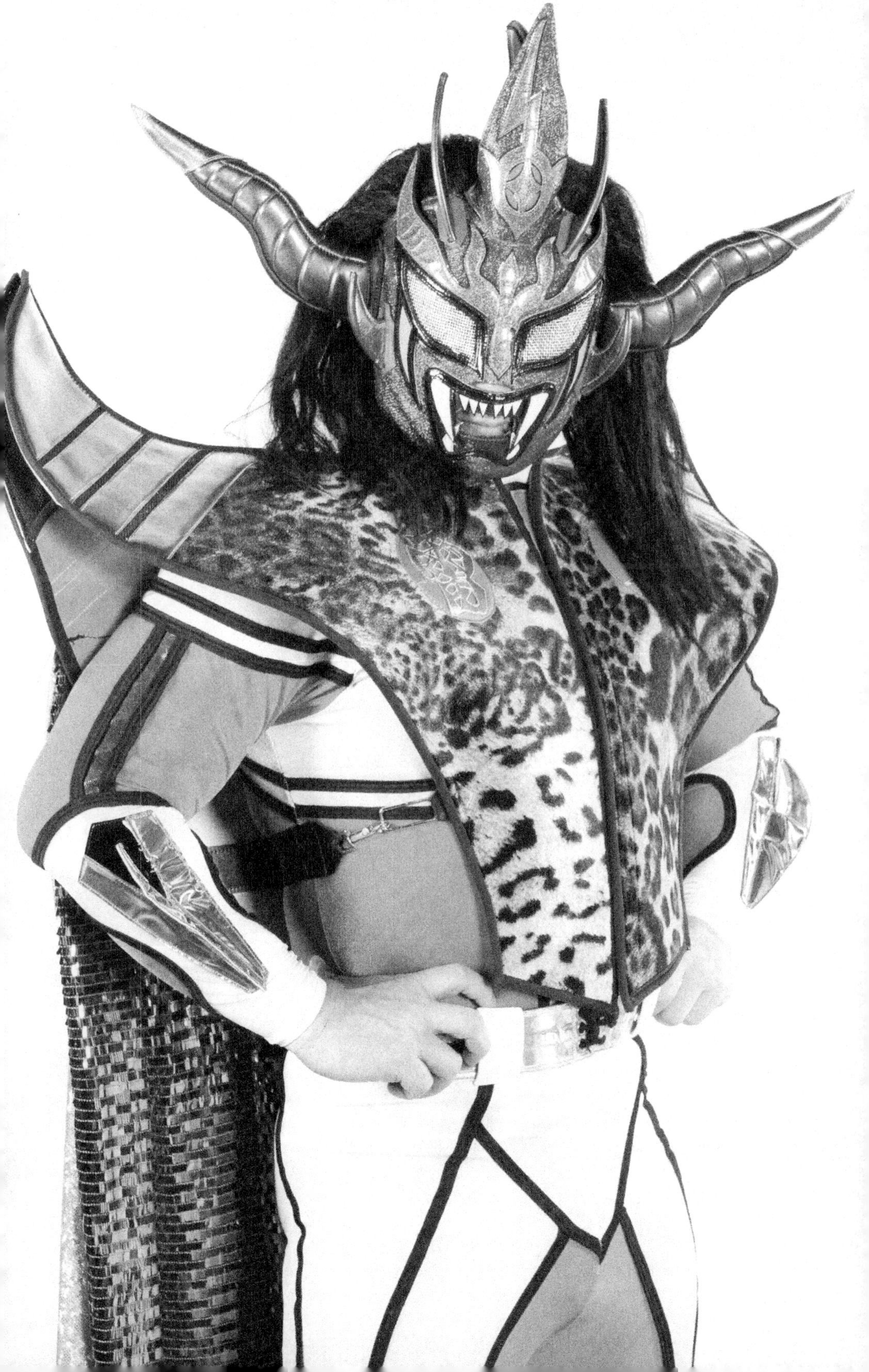

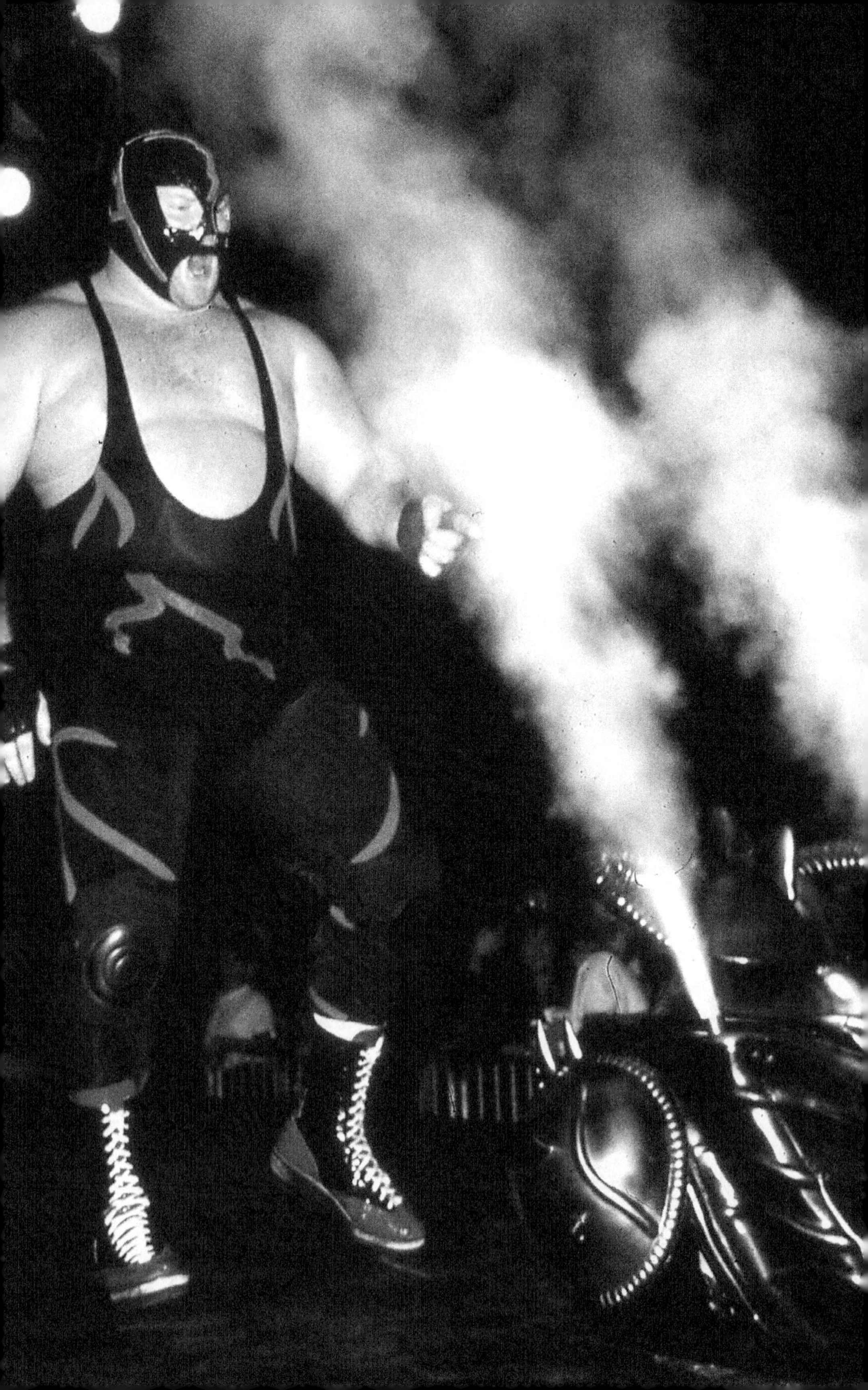

CHAPTER ELEVEN

Lethal Lottery

(Answers: P. 226)

1. Between its founding in February 1997 and final deactivation in July 2002, how many Europeans won the WWF European Championship?

2. The names of Jody Hamilton, Dusty Rhodes, and Gorilla Monsoon have been used by various promotions for what?

3. True or false? Former WWE 'Vaudevillain' Simon Gotch holds a victory over AJPW and Pro Wrestling NOAH legend Mitsuharu Misawa.

4. Who is the only man in wrestling history to have won championships in WWE, WCW, AEW, ECW, and NJPW?

5. What family name links wrestlers Gary Albright, L.A. Smooth, and Naomi?

6. What do the following wrestling-related names have in common: Moppy, Mitch, Head, and Pepé?

7. A fragment of papyrus discovered in Egypt dating back to AD 267, describing a wrestling match between teenagers Nicantinous and Demetrius, is believed to be evidence of the first occurrence of what in the sport?

8. 'Blue eye' is British wrestling slang for what sort of wrestler?

THE ULTIMATE WRESTLING QUIZ BOOK

9. Which of the following men has the best win percentage in their WWE career, standing at 91.7%

    a) The Ultimate Warrior   **b)** El Torito
    c) Hulk Hogan   **d)** Roddy Piper

10. Name the long-running UK-based wrestling magazine which began circulation in 1991 as *Superstars of Wrestling*, and ceased publication in 2014?

11. Which wrestler's name is used as a metaphor for a member of a tag team who achieves less than their partner in singles competition following a break-up?

12. Who composed WWE's in-house music from 1985 until 2017, producing classic entrance themes for the likes of Bret Hart, Shawn Michaels, and Steve Austin?

13. What was the name of the WWE video game which featured no wrestling at all, but rather pitted the organisation's superstars against one another in vehicular combat?

14. What cosmetic change did WWE champions The Miz, Triple H, and Jinder Mahal all make before they won the top title?

15. In 1997, WWE added a 70-foot video wall to the set of *Monday Night Raw* known as what?

LETHAL LOTTERY

16. Who were the cover stars of the first issue of *Pro Wrestling Illustrated*, published September 1979?

17. Which of the following men was the youngest when winning their first wrestling world championship?

    a) Tommy Rich   **b)** Randy Orton
    c) Lou Thesz   **d)** Brock Lesnar

18. In the early days of *SmackDown*'s conception, WWE mooted the possibility of the show being exclusive for which section of their roster?

19. How many of the winners of WWE's King of the Ring tournament between 1985 and 2002 were either former or future WWE World Champions?

20. How does a match said to have went to a 'broadway' end?

21. Who competed in more matches at Madison Square Garden throughout their career, Bret Hart or Hulk Hogan?

22. Who was omitted from video game WCW/nWo Revenge following his suspension by Eric Bischoff for breach of contract?

23. True or false? WWE have promoted more 'Great American Bash' events than either NWA or WCW.

24. What 1963 match is the most watched televised event in Japanese history, and believed to be the most watched wrestling match of all time?

THE ULTIMATE WRESTLING QUIZ BOOK

25. *The Wrestling Observer*'s 'Promotion of the Year' category, awarded to the best wrestling organisation, began in 1983. In what year did WWE win the award for the first time?

26. What important in-ring role links Masao Hattori, Jack Doan, and Brian Hildebrand?

27. Which of the following media franchises do *not* have wrestling video games based on them?

        a) The Simpsons   b) Popeye
        c) Def Jam   d) South Park

28. *Inside Wrestling*, *Ben Strong Wrestling*, and *Pro Wrestling Illustrated* were all wrestling magazines edited by which tenured wrestling journalist?

29. True or false? David Arquette is the only former WCW World Heavyweight Champion to *not* appear on WWE television at least once, either before or after he won the belt.

30. By the end of his career, Shawn Michaels was known by WWE as 'Mr. WrestleMania'. What was his win-loss record at the event?

31. At 3'7", who was the shortest superstar in WWE history?

32. Japanese manga artist Go Nagai is credited with creating the concept of Jushin Liger and which other '80s AJPW star?

LETHAL LOTTERY

33. True or false? Hulk Hogan lost to Jacques Rougeau at the latter's Montreal retirement show in 1997, despite being WCW's top star at time.

34. What was the name of WWE's behind-the-scenes magazine show, which aired between 2002 and 2004?

35. New York Penn Station, the Mirage Nightclub, and All-Star Café were all host venues of which late-night WWE broadcast?

36. 2009's 'Hulkamania: Let the Battle Begin' tour marked the first time Hulk Hogan had wrestled in which country?

37. Who was the first of WWE's inherited WCW superstars to appear on their television programming following the company's buyout in 2001?

38. Under what name did Gorilla Monsoon appear alongside Sean Mooney and Bobby Heenan on 1994's short-lived Baltimore daytime show, *Bingo Break*?

THE ULTIMATE WRESTLING QUIZ BOOK

39. What was the prison number of WWE's ex-convict character, Nailz?

40. Who or what was a regular feature on WWE *SmackDown* between 2001 and 2008, standing 17 feet tall and weighing 6000lbs?

41. Which of the following Minnesotan wrestlers did NOT attend Robbinsdale High School?

    a) John Nord   **b)** Road Warrior Hawk
    c) Curt Hennig **d)** Wayne Bloom

42. Who is the only owner of an NBA championship ring to also win a championship in WWE?

43. In 1993, a set of tag teams faced one another on WWF and WCW pay-per-views. Who were they?

44. What was the first WrestleMania main event in which all participants wrestled under their birth name?

45. '1-chome-3-61 Koraku, Bunkyo City, Tokyo' is the address of which famous wrestling venue?

46. At a total of 448 days, who holds the longest-reign with WWF's second version of the Light Heavyweight Championship, active between 1997 and 2002?

47. What is the only match to take place on both WrestleMania and Starrcade?

48. Seth Rollins vs. Dean Ambrose at Hell in a Cell 2014 was the first time a WWE pay-per-view was main evented by two wrestlers in their twenties since which show?

LETHAL LOTTERY

49. Which of the following were *not* members of the nWo?

    a) Louie Spicolli   **b)** Torrie Wilson
    c) April Hunter   **d)** Miss Hancock

50. By winning the IGF version of the IWGP Heavyweight Championship in June 2007, Kurt Angle became the first man to have held the NWA World Heavyweight, IWGP Heavyweight, and WWE Championships. Who is the only other wrestler to accomplish this feat?

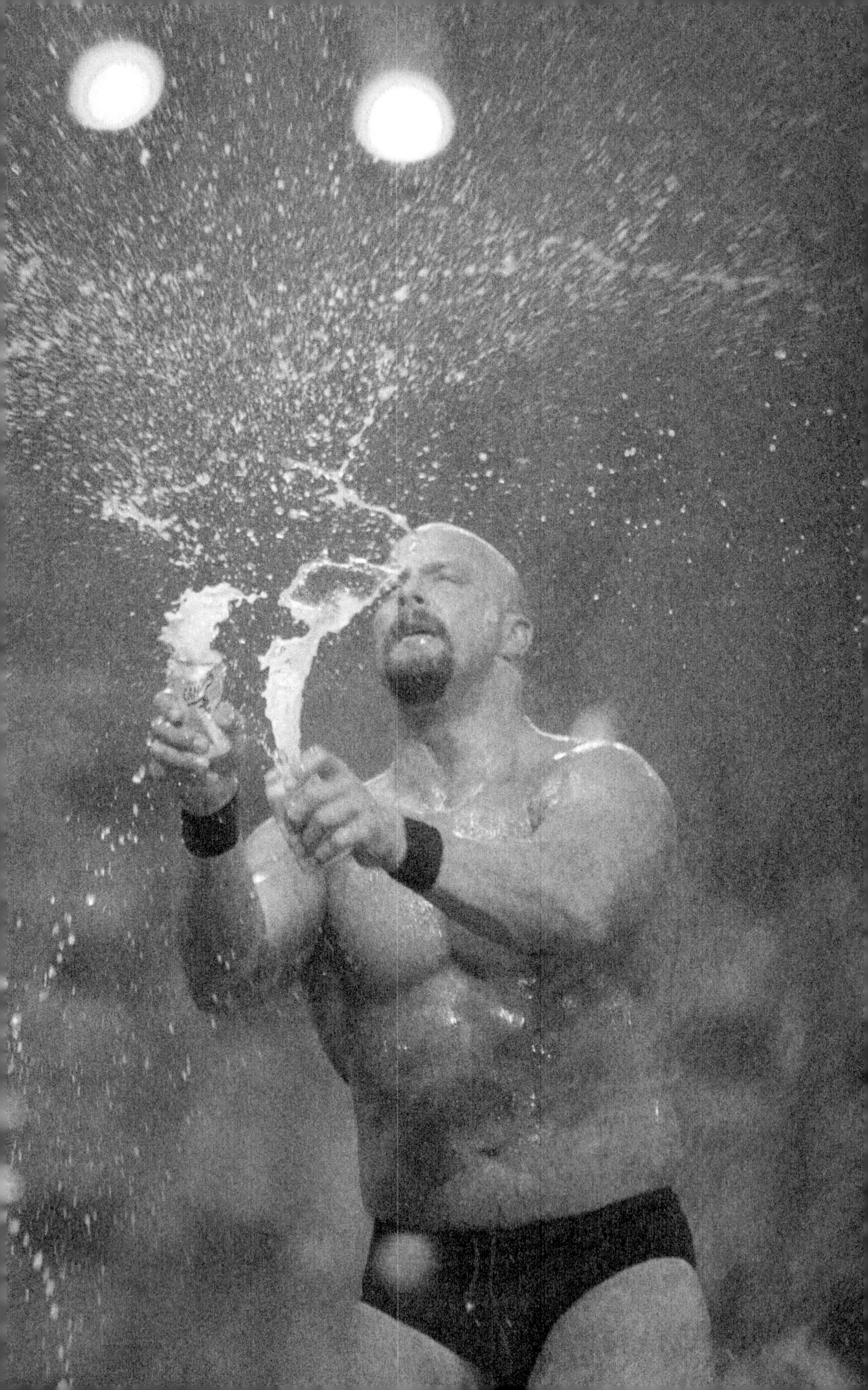

Answers: The Pioneers

1. 'Strangler'

2. Abraham Lincoln

3. 32

4. Martin 'Farmer' Burns

5. Frank Gotch

6. The Highland Games

7. The bear hug

8. Championship belt. The 'diamond belt' claimed by McLaughlin was made of gold and diamonds, and was said to be worth a princely $3,000.

9. True

10. Queen Victoria

11. Australia

12. A champagne glass

13. Tobacco

14. American Heavyweight Championship

15. *An oak (he was known as 'The German Oak').*

16. *Iron Brew (Irn Bru)*

17. *Greece*

18. *Hookers*

19. *She became the first recognised women's World Wrestling champion.*

20. *5 hours*

21. *Zbyszko*

22. *The Gold Dust Trio*

23. *False. Bruce Lee is believed to have followed the regimen of Gama.*

24. *The Masked Marvel*

25. *Wayne Munn (c) vs. Stanislaus Zbyszko. Because of his popularity in American football, Munn was pushed by the Gold Dust Trio as wrestling's next star, despite having almost no wrestling acumen. The Trio booked Munn to beat Zbyszko to build up his credibility, but it backfired when the challenger, having accepted a payoff from rival promoter Tony Stecher, legitimately pinned the champion. Munn's lack of shoot experience left him defenceless.*

26. *Solid Man*

27. *The French Angel*

28. *McMahon*

ANSWERS: THE PIONEERS

29. *False. The World Heavyweight Wrestling Championship was established in 1905. It was preceded by the American Heavyweight Championship, est. 1881.*

30. *All-in*

31. *EMLL*

32. *The Irish Whip*

33. *The sleeperhold*

34. *16 years old*

35. *A steel cage match*

36. *A headlock*

37. *Ali Baba*

38. *Madison Square Garden*

39. *Frank Sinatra*

40. *The Brain*

41. *The Man of 1,000 Holds*

42. *True*

43. *Lancashire*

44. *Estonia*

45. *Greyhound racing, courtesy of his dogs Gangster and Just Andrew, inducted 1964 and 1975, respectively.*

46. *West Point*

47. *That it was fake*

48. *Gorgeous George*

49. *The National Wrestling Alliance*

50. *False. Hollywood Wrestling began airing in 1947, whilst Wrestling from Marigold launched in 1949.*

Answers: The Territories

1. Capitol Wrestling Corporation

2. Orville Brown

3. Bobo Brazil

4. Dallas, TX

5. Verne Gagne

6. Stampede Wrestling

7. The Cow Palace

8. Jim Crockett Promotions

9. True. Lawler held championships on 168 occasions throughout his career, none of which were under WWE's banner.

10. Belgium

11. Pinkie

12. 2,803

13. Wrestling at the Chase

14. Ray Stevens

15. *Buddy Rogers*

16. *Three*

17. *1,468lbs*

18. *True. After Ted's handler and 'promoter' Dave McKigney skipped out on a deal to pay construction worker Ed Williams $1,500 to fight the bear, the would-be challenger swore out a warrant of attachment. Lowndes County jail took Ted as security, later releasing him on a $3,000 bond after McKigney agreed to appear in court.*

19. *Édouard Carpentier*

20. *Hawaii*

21. *Danny Hodge*

22. *'The Crusher'*

23. *Mr. Wrestling II*

24. *Pat O'Connor vs. Buddy Rogers (2-out-of-3 falls)*

25. *True*

26. *Killer Kowalski*

27. *Poffo*

28. *True. Mark 'The Undertaker' Calaway was born in 1965, the same year Funk began working for his father's Western States Sports in Amarillo, TX.*

29. *Mildred Burke*

30. *The Cauliflower Alley Club*

ANSWERS: THE TERRITORIES

31. Harley Race

32. A fork

33. The battle flag of the Confederate Army

34. Sabu

35. The Saint

36. True

37. 10lbs

38. The Fabulous Kangaroos

39. The Destroyer

40. Paul Boesch

41. The Grand Wizard

42. They all slammed Andre the Giant. WWE latterly claimed that Hogan repeating the feat at WrestleMania III was the first time anybody had ever accomplished it.

43. Great Balls of Fire

44. Peter Thornley

45. Lance. After Mike Von Erich was ruled out of the Von Erichs-Freebirds feud of 1985, his father Fritz put William Vaughan in his place, billing him as the son of his fictional brother Waldo.

46. False. It was named after Karl Gotch. Despite being billed as a German menace, Von Raschke was actually born in Omaha, NE.

47. *Mil Máscaras*

48. *False. Whilst Strongbow was an Italian-American with no Native American heritage, McDaniel was of American Choctaw-Chickasaw lineage.*

49. *Ellison (Mary Lillian and Barbara)*

50. *Rio de Janiero, Brazil*

51. *True*

52. *1983*

53. *George Steele*

54. *Valiant*

55. *Austin Idol*

56. *False. They are no relation to one another.*

57. *Bob Armstrong*

58. *Tearing telephone books in half*

59. *Greg Gagne*

60. *False. He was known throughout the territories as Red River Jack and The Masked Marauder.*

61. *Freddie Blassie*

62. *The Briscos, Jack (Freddie Joe) and Gerald (Floyd)*

63. *True. He worked with his father, who was a miner in Brynmawr for 51 years.*

64. *Dr. Jerry Graham*

ANSWERS: THE TERRITORIES

65. *Gordon Solie*

66. *Bearcat*

67. *Ernie Ladd*

68. *Samuel Beckett*

69. *Stan Hansen*

70. *A ban on wearing masks in public.*

71. *The Spoiler; the above ban was only lifted for Máscaras.*

72. *False. He was attacked by a fan wielding a knife dipped in pig fat.*

73. *Joint Promotions*

74. *Alex Karras*

75. *He became the first wrestler to win the company's 'Triple Crown' of World, Intercontinental, and Tag Team Championships.*

76. *Dick the Bruiser*

77. *Mid-South Wrestling*

78. *Shea Stadium*

79. *Big Daddy and Giant Haystacks*

80. *St. Louis Wrestling Club*

81. *Kansas City*

82. *Portland, OR*

83. *All of them.*
84. *Wide*
85. *Andre the Giant*
86. *Parts Unknown*
87. *True. He was named after his father.*
88. *Dominican Republic*
89. *Jackie Pallo*
90. *Bill Dundee*
91. *Rocky III*
92. *Another One Bites the Dust*
93. *Tiger Mask*
94. *True*
95. *Parade of Champions*
96. *Dusty Rhodes*
97. *Terry Gordy*
98. *Backlund's manager, Arnold Skaaland, threw in the towel for the champion.*
99. *Johnny Rodz*
100. *Gino Hernandez*

Answers: The Golden Era

1. WrestleMania. A common misconception is that The Wrestling Classic, the first WWF event widely available on pay-per-view, was the company's first through the medium. The first WrestleMania, whilst largely transmitted via closed-circuit television, could in fact be bought on PPV in some markets.

2. Girls Just Want to Have Fun

3. Nick Bockwinkel

4. Andy Kaufman

5. Antonio Inoki

6. A Flare for the Gold. (Flare was not spelled 'Flair', as in 'Ric Flair', for unknown reasons.)

7. All American Wrestling

8. True

9. $25,000

10. Black Saturday

11. He hit reporter John Stossel after the journalist accused wrestling of being fake.

12. McDonald's

13. *Leilani Kai*

14. *Green*

15. *Bobby Heenan*

16. *False. The match was held in Singapore.*

17. *Bob Backlund*

18. *Jack Reynolds*

19. *He was the main event's special guest timekeeper*

20. *$15,000*

21. *The Iron Sheik*

22. *Nikolai Volkoff*

23. *Honky Tonk Man asked fans for a 'vote of confidence'. After receiving overwhelmingly negative feedback in response, WWF turned the character heel.*

24. *False. Pro Wrestling Illustrated's Lords of the Ring: Superstars and Superbouts, released 1985, was the first.*

25. *The Dingo Warrior*

26. *Highlander*

27. *Sergeant (Sgt. Slaughter)*

28. *$1 million*

29. *Ric Flair*

ANSWERS: THE GOLDEN ERA

30. Dan Spivey

31. New York, Illinois, California

32. A boxing match

33. Fuji Vice

34. The Flower Shop

35. The Islanders dognapped The Bulldog's mascot, Matilda.

36. 93,173. The actual attendance is believed to be around 78,000.

37. Jerry McDevitt

38. Survivor Series

39. Jim Duggan

40. The Islanders (Haku & Tama) vs. The Young Stallions (Paul Roma & Jim Powers) in a two-out-of-three-falls match

41. Bruno Sammartino

42. One Man Gang

43. 31 seconds

44. He stabbed Rhodes with one of his shoulder spikes.

45. Jake Roberts' wife, Cheryl

46. Boris Zhukov

47. 'The American Dream' Dusty Rhodes

48. *The Ghetto Blaster*

49. *Italy*

50. *WWF Canadian Championship*

51. *A macaw (parrot)*

52. *AWA. The company invented a title change in Albuquerque, NM, in which Scott Hall & Curt Hennig (pictured) beat champions Jimmy Garvin & the departed Regal.*

53. *Rip Thomas*

54. *Pat Patterson*

55. *They were all managed by Freddie Blassie*

56. *Barry Manilow*

57. *An 'X', in reference to cultist Charles Manson.*

58. *Jesse Ventura*

59. *False. The Ultimate Warrior vs. Rick Rude headlined SummerSlam '90.*

60. *'Winged Eagle'*

61. *Bee*

62. *WWF The Main Event, during which Andre the Giant defeated Hulk Hogan for the WWF World Heavyweight Championship.*

63. *Riki Choshu*

64. *Road Warrior Hawk*

ANSWERS: THE GOLDEN ERA

65. *The Bushwhackers*
66. *Ric Flair vs. Sting*
67. *The Yamazaki Corporation*
68. *Universal Wrestling Corporation*
69. *Pizza Hut*
70. *Spartacus*
71. *SuperClash III*
72. *The U.S. Express*
73. *Rheingans' Renegades*
74. *'The Mega-Powers Explode!'*
75. *True. She was the first woman in the state of Missouri to do so.*
76. *Arrogance*
77. *Mr. Perfect*
78. *Tully Blanchard*
79. *Six*
80. *The Toronto SkyDome*
81. *Diamond Dallas Page*
82. *The Million Dollar Championship (Ted DiBiase defeated Jake Roberts via countout).*
83. *Beefcake had been involved in a parasailing accident.*

84. Héctor Guerrero

85. Los Angeles Memorial Coliseum

86. Jimmy Snuka

87. Five

88. True. They attended the same high school.

89. Shaker Heights

90. This Tuesday in Texas

91. Snake meat; Earthquake fashioned the meal from Jake Roberts' snake, Damien.

92. The Junkyard Dog

93. Three

94. He was caught blading on screen. Bret Hart also bladed on the show, but was too discreet to be caught.

95. KAYFABE

96. The Hells Angels

97. Randy Colley

98. MicroLeague Wrestling

99. Saskatoon, Canada

100. UK Rampage

ANSWERS: A NEW GENERATION

1. One (The Natural Disasters & The Nasty Boys vs. Money Inc. & The Beverly Brothers)

2. 'Grand Champion'

3. USS Intrepid

4. Rob Bartlett

5. Max Moon

6. Finkus Maximus

7. Earl

8. Eddie Gilbert

9. Steve Keirn. Ray Apollo adopted the Doink gimmick after Borne left the company, and Steve Lombardi portrayed the clown on an October 2005 episode of Raw. Dusty Wolfe regularly played the character on independent shows throughout North America.

10. WCW International World Heavyweight Championship

11. Bob Backlund

12. Mortal Kombat

13. 2 Cold Scorpio

14. *False. Bigelow received a bye to the final after Tatanka and Lex Luger went to a time-limit draw in their quarter-final.*

15. *A Rest in Peace match*

16. *His red hair*

17. *His 'main squeeze'*

18. *A stock car*

19. *Dreamer poked a lit cigarette into his eye.*

20. *Two: Jacques (Canada) and Ludvig Borga (Finland)*

21. *Barry Horowitz*

22. *True.*

23. *The Undertaker*

24. *The White Castle of Fear*

25. *Adam Bomb*

26. *Whoomp! (There it is)*

27. *The Great Kabuki*

28. *An electric guitar (pictured: Man Mountain Rock)*

29. *James Dudley*

30. *They all held doctorates ('Dr. Death' Steve Williams, 'Doctor of Style' Slick, and Dr. Harvey Wippleman)*

31. *Blackjack Brawl*

ANSWERS: A NEW GENERATION

32. Vader

33. Bash at the Beach '94

34. Mike 'IRS' Rotundo, who made a cameo in the crowd alongside an actor portraying Bill Clinton. He was also shown backstage ahead of a planned ten-man tag team match that was ultimately bumped from the show.

35. A toupée

36. Art Donovan

37. 84 years old

38. Leslie Nielsen

39. Sione (occasionally spelled Seone)

40. Mr. T

41. Bunkhouse Buck

42. Bob Backlund

43. Blackburn Rovers (or 'the Blackburn Rovers', as he stated)

44. The Mall of America

45. False. In 2003, Tony 'Ludvig Borga' Halme became a member of the Finnish Parliament representing far-right populist party True Finns.

46. Jenny McCarthy

47. A new house in Orlando, FL

48. A soccer player

49. ECW

50. A sumo monster truck match

51. Hogan 'accidentally' pushed The Giant off the roof.

52. A gold chain

53. Jean LaFitte

54. False. Diesel's run was interrupted by Bret Hart vs. British Bulldog at In Your House 5.

55. Cape Fear

56. Two Dudes with Attitudes

57. Wrestling Challenge

58. 'Ain't I Great?'

59. Great White North

60. White paper/ blank paper

61. Bertha Faye

62. Avalanche. John 'Avalanche' Tenta was, however, a member of the Dungeon under his second WCW gimmick, 'The Shark'.

63. Roddy Piper

64. Cold Killer

65. 0-0

ANSWERS: A NEW GENERATION

66. He was a refuse technician (a garbage man).

67. Sexton Hardcastle

68. Marlene Dietrich

69. Four: The Bodydonnas, The Godwinns, The Smoking Gunns, and Legion of Doom 2000.

70. Mantaur

71. South Carolina

72. Steve Doll and The Mauler

73. John 3:16

74. "I respect you, booker man!"

75. None

76. True. According to Eric Bischoff, Sting had agreed to turn heel for the role, only for Hulk Hogan to call up and put his own name forward.

77. Ahmed Johnson

78. Sioux City, IO

79. November to Remember

80. Terry Gordy

81. 3.0

82. Tekno Team 2000 (pictured: Troy (Erik Watts) and Travis (Chad Fortune))

83. Taz

84. The Nation of Islam

85. The Environment

86. The Rock

87. Renegade

88. Frying pans

89. WWF Women's Championship. Debra 'Alundra Blayze' Miceli left WWF with the belt in December 1995. She joined WCW later that month, dropping the title into a trash can on an episode of Monday Nitro.

90. Sturgis Motorcycle Rally

91. Abismo Negro. He featured in a dark six-man tag team match before the show.

92. Nadine and Tracy

93. Sycho Sid

94. 'Heat!'

95. Mr. Hughes. He was replaced by Chyna.

96. Souled Out

97. Steve Austin vs. Bret Hart (WrestleMania 13)

98. 35

99. Rick Rude. An hour after showing up on Nitro with just a mustache, Rude appeared with a full beard on the pre-taped episode of Raw.

100. The Simpsons

ANSWERS: ATTITUDE

1. *Steve Austin.*
2. *Boston Brawl*
3. *In Your House: No Way Out of Texas*
4. *Savio Vega*
5. *Chris Adams vs. Randy Savage*
6. *'Bombastic' (Bob) and 'Bodacious' (Bart)*
7. *As a special guest referee for match between Larry Zbyszko and Eric Bischoff*
8. *A jeep (not, as WWE have repeated ever since, a tank).*
9. *Owen Hart*
10. *True*
11. *A stop sign*
12. *Seinfeld*
13. *Arm drag*
14. *TV-14*
15. *Truth and Consequences*

16. Droz

17. $75,000

18. The New Age Outlaws

19. Land of the Rising Venis

20. Chae

21. Humanitarian of the Year

22. Chyna

23. South Park's Eric Cartman

24. Southern Justice

25. $3.5 million

26. Karl Malone

27. Supply and Demand

28. Mankind

29. Steve Austin and The Rock (Mr. McMahon sent out henchman Boss Man twice, to both eliminate Austin and lie down for The Rock).

30. 173-0

31. Chad Fortune

32. Have a Nice Day! A Tale of Blood and Sweatsocks

33. Big Boss Man

34. Capital Carnage

ANSWERS: ATTITUDE

35. One Warrior Nation
36. Just Over Broke
37. 500,000
38. Beyond the Mat
39. Chyna
40. A chicken
41. St. Valentine's Day Massacre
42. Kurt Angle
43. Detroit River
44. Michael Cole and Jim Cornette
45. 'The Ragin' Climax'
46. 35 seconds
47. Chris Jericho
48. Miss Madness
49. It came in a tag team match against Sting & Kevin Nash
50. Richard Petty
51. 43 years
52. A whistle
53. Lance Storm and Justin Credible
54. Carl Ouellet

55. *Super Astros*

56. *Meat*

57. *Shane McMahon's travel bag. McMahon told Mideon he could keep the belt after he found it.*

58. *False. He wrestled five times (vs. The Big Show, Kane, Mideon & Viscera, Mankind, and The Rock).*

59. *Pete Gas, Joey Abs, and Rodney*

60. *'Allegedly well over 400lbs'*

61. *Brian Adams*

62. *Bill Busch*

63. *Double D*

64. *Mae Young exposed her breasts (she was wearing a prosthesis).*

65. *False. Wim Ruska, who won two Judo gold medals for the Netherlands in 1972, made numerous WWF appearances in the late '70s.*

66. *Naked Mideon*

67. *A hand*

68. *Muffy*

69. *He urinated in it*

70. *Neither man was contracted to the company. Awesome had left for WCW whilst still ECW World Heavyweight Champion. Taz was 'borrowed' from WWF to win the belt off him.*

ANSWERS: ATTITUDE

71. The Kat and Terri Runnels
72. Elizabeth
73. 10
74. Essa Rios
75. 6-5
76. Los Conquistadores
77. Trish Stratus
78. The Parents Television Council
79. A leather jacket
80. Jim Duggan
81. Eric Bischoff
82. WCW World Television Championship
83. Drew Carey
84. The Barbarian. Meng left WCW with the belt, and gave it to his close friend during an independent event on 21 January 2001.
85. Bull Buchanan
86. Fusient Media Ventures
87. $4.2 million
88. Jeff Jarrett
89. Mike Tenay and Scott Hudson

90. Two: Sgt. Slaughter and eventual winner The Iron Sheik

91. $4 (four dollars)

92. False. It was Greed.

93. The Rock

94. ECW

95. Yuji Nagata

96. No Limit Soldiers

97. Air Paris

98. Kane

99. Sheffield

100. Slayer

Answers: The Monopoly

1. True
2. Scott Hudson and Arn Anderson
3. Booker T
4. Sara
5. Freddie Blassie
6. KroniK
7. Lita and Torrie Wilson
8. Josh Matthews
9. Vengeance
10. World Wildlife Fund
11. False. It was concocted during a fishing trip.
12. He was a deacon.
13. Tennessee State Fairgrounds Sports Arena
14. 114
15. John Cena

THE ULTIMATE WRESTLING QUIZ BOOK

16. Scott Steiner

17. 48

18. He was gifted it by Eric Bischoff.

19. Intercontinental Championship

20. Texas Wrestling Alliance

21. S.H.I.T. (Superhero in Training)

22. Yokozuna, who was 26 years old when he won the WWF Championship at WrestleMania IX.

23. 'The SmackDown Six'

24. Nailz

25. Jésus

26. They were voted for by fans online.

27. Five

28. False

29. A shooting star press

30. Nathan Jones

31. Thuggin' and Buggin' Enterprises

32. Charlie Haas and Rikishi

33. Survivor Series 2002

34. False. He graduated from Harvard.

35. Lance Cade and René Duprée

ANSWERS: THE MONOPOLY

36. The Hilton
37. False. The Rock accomplished the feat in November 1998.
38. Triple H
39. The Great American Bash
40. He was entombed in concrete by The Undertaker.
41. Ohio Valley Wrestling
42. Batista
43. Mark Jindrak
44. CNBC
45. Scotty 2 Hotty
46. True
47. A kimono
48. Juventud
49. New Year's Revolution 2006
50. It was the first WrestleMania with no form of tag team match.
51. Senshi
52. 'Disasterpieces'
53. A lawnmower
54. True

55. The Undertaker and The Big Show. Khali was ruled out of his signature match due to heightened liver enzymes.

56. Sharmell

57. Kane

58. James Mitchell

59. Worms

60. Lockdown

61. Muhammad Hassan

62. Wakinyan

63. Shillelagh

64. 'The end'

65. Impact!

66. AJ Styles vs. Samoa Joe vs. Christopher Daniels

67. The Condemned

68. Ernest 'The Cat' Miller. Brodus Clay would later adopt the theme as his own.

69. 90,000

70. Bobby Lashley, The Big Show, Test, Hardcore Holly, Rob Van Dam, and CM Punk

71. To get into the ring.

ANSWERS: THE MONOPOLY

72. None (Dusty Rhodes, Curt Hennig, Jerry Lawler, Nick Bockwinkel, Mr. Fuji, The Sheik, Jim Ross)

73. His teeth

74. Matt can speak conversational Spanish.

75. Louisville, KY - the location of WWE's developmental territory, OVW.

76. A pink slip

77. A Jingle with Jillian'

78. True

79. Akebono

80. The Rock 'n' Rave Infection

81. Antonio and Romeo

82. Terry Gordy

83. Bobby Lashley

84. The Silver Surfer

85. Hornswoggle

86. True:
    - w/ Shawn Michaels vs. Batista & The Undertaker (No Way Out)
    - vs. Shawn Michaels (WrestleMania 23)
    - vs. Shawn Michaels vs. Edge vs. Randy Orton (Backlash)
    - vs. The Great Khali (Judgment Day)
    - vs. The Great Khali (One Night Stand)

- *vs. Bobby Lashley vs. Mick Foley vs. Rand Orton vs. King Booker (Vengeance: Night of Champions)*
- *vs. Bobby Lashley (The Great American Bash)*
- *vs. Randy Orton (SummerSlam)*

87. True. He was shown in the crowd as the sponsor of WrestleManias IV and V, had a ringside seat for WrestleMania VII, and conducted an awkward interview with Jesse Ventura at WrestleMania XX.

88. MVP

89. Cherry

90. True. He was part of a six-man tag team match with AJ Styles and Petey Williams against Milano Collection AT, Minoru, & Prince Devitt.

91. Michelle Williams

92. $141^{2/3}\%$

93. Bryan Danielson

94. "I'm sorry. I love you."

95. He had no music or TitanTron video.

96. Night of Champions

97. McMahon's Million Dollar Mania

98. Rick Astley's 'Never Gonna Give You Up'

99. 888. The number was a cipher for 'HHH' (H is the 8th letter of the alphabet).

100. The company moved from a TV-14 rating to TV-PG.

Answers: The PG Era

1. Robert 'Gorilla Monsoon' Marella
2. Shawn Michaels' wife, Rebecca
3. The Shawshank Redemption
4. Just Too Gangsta
5. Tony Atlas
6. The Miz and John Morrison
7. Lara Croft
8. Three (vs. Mark Henry, Chavo Guerrero, and The Big Show)
9. 'Kung Fu Naki'
10. Abraham Lincoln and George Washington (Abraham Washington)
11. Randy 'The Ram' Robinson
12. They were all multi-generational superstars.
13. Jenna Morasca vs. Sharmell
14. His pyrotechnics exploded in his face.

15. *Drew McIntyre*

16. *Rob Van Dam*

17. *The Brian Kendrick*

18. *False. Kingston, born in Kumasi, Ghana, was the first. Kamala, despite being billed as 'the Ugandan Giant', was born in Oxford, MS.*

19. *One second*

20. *Carny. The jargon uses an infix, 'iz', in words, hence 'K-iz-arny' ('Karny' + 'iz').*

21. *A border guard*

22. *Mike Knox*

23. *Kid Rock*

24. *66 years old. He eclipsed the record set by Fabulous Moolah, who was 62 when she faced Velvet McIntyre at WrestleMania 2.*

25. *'Miss. WrestleMania'*

26. *The Whole F'n Show*

27. *The Bash*

28. *Teddy Hart*

29. *The Real World*

30. *A butterfly*

31. *'SummerFest'*

ANSWERS: THE PG ERA

32. Aksana

33. True (3-2). It was awarded to Ted DiBiase in 1989 (by himself), his protégé The Ringmaster in 1995, and his son Ted DiBiase Jr. in 2010. In that time, only Virgil and DiBiase won the belt in the ring, trading it back and forth in 1991.

34. Tiffany

35. Three

36. "Faith!"

37. SmackDown 2-1 Raw

38. False

39. 'Dolph Diggler'

40. Jesse Ventura

41. The Bellas and The Colóns

42. Wembley Arena

43. True (The Miz, Drew McIntyre, Jack Swagger, Sheamus)

44. Beth Phoenix

45. They stopped using a six-sided ring.

46. An eagle. Chavo was the 'Swagger Soaring Eagle'. His uncle, Hector, was under the turkey suit of The Gobbledy Gooker at Survivor Series '90.

47. Shawn Michaels. 'Hacksaw' Jim Duggan joined this exclusive club in 2012.

THE ULTIMATE WRESTLING QUIZ BOOK

48. Jeff Hardy. He made his return to the company on this show.

49. Bret Hart and Shawn Michaels

50. True. The show averaged 2.2 million viewers, beating the previous best of 1.97 million.

51. The Miz

52. Elimination Chamber

53. Cody Rhodes

54. Alcohol, tobacco, and drugs

55. 13 years

56. Sheamus

57. True (Mark Henry, The Miz, Big Show, Randy Orton, Jack Swagger, Christian, Dolph Ziggler, Drew Mcintyre, Kane, Kofi Kingston, Triple H, Sheamus, Rey Mysterio, CM Punk, Bret Hart, Mr. McMahon, Chris Jericho, Edge, John Cena, Batista, The Undertaker, Shawn Michaels))

58. 'Word Up'

59. WWE Niagara Falls

60. Gypsy Joe

61. 6'8"

62. Fatal 4-Way

63. Roberts' own neck tie

ANSWERS: THE PG ERA

64. *One - Daniel Bryan*

65. *A pig ('Piggie James')*

66. *40*

67. *Diesel*

68. *The Rock*

69. *Michael Cole*

70. *The Corre*

71. *Faceless (lit. 'without face')*

72. *True. At 5'6", Rey was marginally less tall than his friend Eddie Guerrero (5'8"), who won the belt in 2004.*

73. *She eliminated herself on purpose after being told by agents to get eliminated within a minute of the match starting. Kim quit WWE shortly afterwards.*

74. *Johnny Gargano*

75. *True*

76. *Kaval*

77. *Ice cream bars*

78. *Barack Obama*

79. *All American Wrestling*

80. *Kane*

81. *True*

THE ULTIMATE WRESTLING QUIZ BOOK

82. 'Once in a Lifetime'
83. John Cena and The Rock
84. She had flatulence during her promos and segments.
85. 1.2 million
86. Jon Silver (Rob Grymes)
87. 'Stand up for WWE'
88. Santa Claus
89. Sakamoto
90. Brock Lesnar
91. The Funkadactyls
92. False. John Cena won his 2012 cash-in against CM Punk via disqualification, and therefore failed to win the title.
93. Brother-in-law
94. Dr. Shelby
95. Full Sail University
96. True
97. "We the People"
98. Total Divas
99. WWE and World Heavyweight Championships
100. WWE Classics on Demand

ANSWERS: THE NETWORK

1. *The Wyatt Family*

2. *Batista*

3. *Rey Mysterio*

4. *Cesaro vs. Sami Zayn*

5. *NXT Arrival*

6. *Sheamus*

7. *The SilverDome (the show was taking place at New Orleans' Superdome).*

8. *Snake Bight*

9. *Andre the Giant*

10. *Randy Orton (WrestleMania 21)*

11. *Best in the World. The promotion had produced pre-taped pay-per-views for many years prior, the first of which, Respect is Earned, aired 1 July 2007.*

12. *JBL*

13. *SIERRA-HOTEL-INDIA-ECHO-LIMA-DELTA*

14. *Adrian Neville vs. Tyson Kidd*

15. True. His favourite is a 1967 Green Hornet lunchbox featuring Bruce Lee.
16. Sibling
17. Tyler Breeze
18. The APA and the New Age Outlaws
19. Stardust
20. The Slayers
21. Gainesville, FL
22. 16
23. The Ultimate Warrior
24. Bubba Ray Dudley
25. Paige
26. 'Hero of Pain'
27. #GiveDivasAChance
28. The Easter Rising
29. All of them
30. Wine making
31. King of the Ring 2015
32. Ryogoku Kokugikan (Sumo Hall)
33. A trombone

ANSWERS: THE NETWORK

34. WCW Nitro. She made a brief cameo during a tour of father Ric's home on the 15 May 2000 episode of the show.

35. Jushin Liger (Liger technically appeared for the company at the Wrestling Summit, a show jointly produced by WWF, NJPW, and AJPW in 1990, on which he faced Akira Nogami.)

36. The Submission Sorority

37. False. He finished 10th in 2013.

38. Alberto Del Rio

39. Dusty Rhodes

40. United Kingdom

41. Gary Neville

42. Sami Zayn

43. William Shatner

44. Jakked. He was beaten by Hurricane Helms on the 26 January 2002 edition of the show.

45. True. Unwilling to upset sponsors by having either man intentionally draw blood through blading, WWE deemed it more sensible to have Lesnar bust Orton open hardway, so it could be played off as accidental.

46. It started airing live.

47. 101,763. Journalist Dave Meltzer reported the attendance was more likely 93,730, the maximum capacity for an event in the stadium excluding personnel.

48. *Emmalina*

49. *Bob Backlund*

50. *Run an orphanage in his native Mexico.*

51. *Eddie Guerrero*

52. *Jacqueline Moore*

53. *The Legacy Wing*

54. *True (Roadblock (12 March) and Roadblock: End of the Line (18 December))*

55. *None*

56. *Blackpool*

57. *Daniel Bryan*

58. *Ricochet*

59. *Cirque du Soleil*

60. *One - he was forced to forfeit the title on the following night's Raw, due to an injury suffered whilst winning it.*

61. *205lbs*

62. *Amped*

63. *To avoid clashing with a presidential debate between Donald Trump and Hillary Clinton.*

64. *Carmella*

65. *Superstar Shake-up*

ANSWERS: THE NETWORK

66. *10 (Dillinger was billed as 'The Perfect 10')*

67. *Spiders*

68. *Señor Benjamin*

69. *Charlotte Flair and Sasha Banks*

70. *War Games*

71. *Occam's Razor (Akam & Rezar)*

72. *Xbox Magazine*

73. *Facebook*

74. *24 (UK Championship Tournament, TakeOver: San Antonio, Royal Rumble, Elimination Chamber, Fastlane, TakeOver: Orlando, WrestleMania 33, Payback, UK Championship Special, TakeOver: Chicago, Backlash, Extreme Rules, Money in the Bank, Great Balls of Fire, Battleground, TakeOver: Brooklyn III, SummerSlam, Mae Young Classic Finale, No Mercy, Hell in a Cell, TLC, TakeOver: War Games, Survivor Series, Clash of Champions)*

75. *Kinshasa, DR Congo. The city was the host of Ali vs. Foreman's 'Rumble in the Jungle', during which fans chanted, "Ali boma ye!", meaning, "Ali, kill him!" in the Lingala language.*

76. *19 years old*

77. *The dialling code of Australia*

78. *The Manhattan Center*

79. *Impact Wrestling*

80. *Elias*

81. *Jason Jordan*

82. *Every day*

83. *John Cone*

84. *Michelle McCool (5)*

85. *The Creation of Adam*

86. *True*

87. *Gorgeous Ladies of Wrestling (GLOW)*

88. *The North American Championship. They were the first winners of both WWE championships bearing the name. DiBiase won the WWF North American Heavyweight Championship in February 1979; Cole bagged the NXT North American Championship in March 2018.*

89. *Administrator of the Small Business Administration*

90. *False. She is the second. Stephanie McMahon won the WWF Women's Championship in March 2000. Her father, Vince, won the WWF Championship in September 1999.*

91. *Two (vs. Triple H (WrestleMania 32) and vs. The Undertaker (WrestleMania 33)*

92. *False. Sheamus (Ireland) won 2012's Royal Rumble match.*

93. *914*

94. *The Fabulous Moolah*

ANSWERS: THE NETWORK

95. Saudi Arabia

96. Hiroki Sumi

97. True. It eclipsed the 2011 Royal Rumble match (69:52).

98. nZo

99. AAA. A TV taping at the Los Angeles Sports Arena on 12 March 1994, headlined by a steel cage match between Konnan and Jake Roberts, drew a reported 13,823 fans.

100. NWA Worlds Heavyweight Championship

Answers:
Being Elite

1. Melbourne, Australia

2. False. LPWA Super Ladies Showdown, held 23 February 1992, was the first.

3. 206 years (The Undertaker (53), Kane (51), Triple-H (49), Shawn Michaels (53))

4. Nia Jax

5. SoCal Uncensored (Christopher Daniels, Frankie Kazarian, and Scorpio Sky)

6. False. It was Dr. Britt Baker

7. Oriental Wrestling Entertainment

8. None

9. Kip Sabian vs. Sammy Guevara

10. Two (Billy Gunn and Tommy Dreamer)

11. Bret Hart

12. AAA World Tag Team Championship

13. The Viking Experience

ANSWERS: BEING ELITE

14. *False. Beth Phoenix, who appeared in the 2010 men's Royal Rumble, also took part in the first-ever women's version.*

15. *The number 30 spot in the respect men's and women's Royal Rumble matches.*

16. *Ricochet*

17. *True (Toni Storm (New Zealand) vs. Rhea Ripley (Australia))*

18. *Yachting*

19. *Worlds Collide*

20. *Hemp*

21. *Halftime Heat*

22. *Mustafa Ali. He was replaced by Kofi Kingston.*

23. *Fyre Festival (Fyter Fest)*

24. *Gun violence*

25. *Colin Jost*

26. *269*

27. *Bad Reputation*

28. *WrestleMania X and WrestleMania 2000*

29. *Alexa Bliss and Natalya*

30. *A giant spider*

31. *Goldberg*

THE ULTIMATE WRESTLING QUIZ BOOK

32. True

33. Stomping Grounds

34. EVOLVE

35. Teal Piper (the daughter of Roddy Piper)

36. The Graveyard Dogs

37. Smackville

38. Big Brother

39. Waylon Mercy

40. Chris Jericho

41. True

42. The match was stopped by the referee after Rollins hit a prone Fiend with a sledgehammer, despite the contest having a no disqualification rule. The Fiend had used a larger hammer of his own earlier in the bout, without reproach from the official.

43. Kabuki

44. TNT

45. Stephen Merchant

46. A clump of their hair

47. False. According to company EVP Cody Rhodes, it is worth $42,000.

48. False. Gable is 5'8". The average height of American men in 2019 was 5'9.5"

ANSWERS: BEING ELITE

49. *Hulk Hogan and Ric Flair*

50. *Tyson Fury*

51. *NXT*

52. *False. General Mustafa (born in Iran) and Col. Adnan (born in Iraq) teamed with Sgt. Slaughter against Hulk Hogan & The Ultimate Warrior at SummerSlam '91.*

53. *Pat Patterson*

54. *True*

55. *10*

56. *The Nightmare Factory*

57. *Challenge for the AEW World Championship*

58. *Tessa Blanchard*

59. *18*

60. *Edge*

61. *Norwegian Pearl*

62. *Prestigious Tuwaiq Mountain Trophy*

63. *Kenny Omega & Adam Page vs. The Young Bucks.*

64. *0. The global COVID-19 pandemic stipulated that no fans could attend.*

65. *False. WrestleMania 2 was held across three venues.*

66. *Andromeda*

THE ULTIMATE WRESTLING QUIZ BOOK

67. Titan Towers (the headquarters of WWE)

68. In Your House

69. 'The Greatest Wrestling Match Ever'

70. Wyatt Swamp Fight

71. The ThunderDome

72. Capitol Wrestling Center

73. Red

74. Mimosa

75. Jacksonville Jaguars

76. Blackjack

77. False. He cut a brief promo at the close of the show.

78. Final Fantasy VII

79. He was set alight and burned alive.

80. India

81. Three

82. 61 years old

83. A weather delay

84. Bad Bunny

85. WrestleMania ('WrestleMania Backlash')

ANSWERS: BEING ELITE

86. True. The Miz, Nikki A.S.H. and Big E all successfully cashed-in contracts. Three attempts were made in 2018, but Braun Strowman failed in his effort against Roman Reigns.

87. Dark Elevation

88. Jungle Boy

89. False. He made a one-off cameo under a mask for Milwaukee's MKE Wrestling in April 2019.

90. Satoshi Kojima

91. SummerSlam '92

92. Game of Thrones ('Winter is Coming')

93. Peacock

94. Sherri Martel

95. 99

96. Arthur Ashe Stadium

97. Ring of Honor

98. Cleopatra's golden egg

99. Bryan Danielson

100. 1 January

ANSWERS: PURORESU

1. Rikidozan

2. Japan Pro Wrestling Alliance (JWA)

3. Antonio Inoki

4. Oddjob (Goldfinger)

5. 'King of Sports'

6. Lou Thesz (vs. Rikidozan for the NWA International Heavyweight Championship on 27 August 1958)

7. International Wrestling Enterprise (IWE)

8. International Wrestling Grand Prix (IWGP)

9. All Japan Pro Wrestling

10. 6'10"

11. Hiro Matsuda

12. A pelican

13. 107

14. WWF World Martial Arts Heavyweight Championship

15. Abdullah the Butcher

ANSWERS: PURORESU

16. True. He defeated Antonio Inoki to win the original version of the belt in June 1983, which was designed to be defended annually against the winner of the IWGP League.

17. Kayfabe

18. Shooto

19. Tiger Driver '85

20. Scott Hall

21. All Japan Women's Pro-Wrestling (AJW)

22. The Crush Gals

23. None - each of them vacated the title.

24. The Tokyo Dome

25. Salman Hashimikov

26. Fighting Spirit Three Musketeers

27. Jumbo Tsuruta

28. The Triple Crown Heavyweight Championship

29. UWF

30. Wrestling Summit

31. Spectacles

32. Super World of Sports

33. Wrestle and Romance

34. 4 January

35. WCW. The first show was named Super Warriors in Tokyo.

36. Sting

37. Greatest 18 Club

38. Mitsuharu Misawa, Kenta Kobashi, Toshiaki Kawada, Akira Taue

39. Pancrase

40. True

41. 'King's Road' ('Odo')

42. 'Charisma of Tears'

43. True (Onita, Mr. Gannosuke & Katsutoshi Niiyama vs. The Gladiator Mike Awesome, Mr Pogo & Hideki Hosaka (25/9/94))

44. Jushin Liger

45. Top of the Super Juniors

46. Hayabusa

47. Red Shoes

48. The bloodiness of a match

49. Kishin Liger

ANSWERS: PURORESU

50. Ten - he combined NJPW's J-Crown, comprised of eight titles, with the NWA World Middleweight Championship and WCW Cruiserweight Championship.

51. Antonio Inoki vs. Don Frye

52. Shark Deathmatch

53. To light a firework up the opponent's bottom.

54. 'Inokism'

55. Aja Kong

56. Motoko Baba

57. Noah

58. Global Honored Crown Heavyweight Championship

59. Bad Ass Translate Trading

60. Mike Barton

61. Masa Chono

62. 25

63. Inoki Genome Federation

64. Kurt Angle and Brock Lesnar

65. Peter Pan

66. Wrestle Kingdom

67. Shinya Hashimoto

THE ULTIMATE WRESTLING QUIZ BOOK

68. *Verdict*

69. *Politics ('Atsushi Onita's Anytime, Anywhere Politics Quiz')*

70. *CHAOS*

71. *Valiantly (New Blood Evolution Valiantly Eternal Radical)*

72. *New Jersey*

73. *Back to the Future's Marty McFly*

74. *'Young Lions'*

75. *False. He only used it seven times, and it was never kicked out of.*

76. *Osaka*

77. *Giant Bernard (Matt Bloom) and Karl Anderson*

78. *Open the Dream Gate Championship*

79. *Final Burning in Budokan*

80. *Hiroshi Tanahashi*

81. *Roppongi (Roppongi Vice)*

82. *Tatsumi Fujinami*

83. *Bad Luck Fale*

84. *Daryl*

85. *Kazuchika Okada*

ANSWERS: PURORESU

86. The championship belt itself
87. IWGP Intercontinental Championship
88. Karl Anderson
89. Kota Ibushi
90. The Golden Lovers
91. 'He' was an inflatable doll.
92. 'Tranquilo'
93. Super Liger
94. False. Ric Flair vs. Ricky Steamboat on 18 March 1989 and Mitsuharu Misawa vs. Toshiaki Kawada on 6 June 1997 both received six-star ratings.
95. World Wonder Ring Stardom
96. NJPW World
97. Kenny Omega
98. Fire Pro Wrestling
99. The All Asia Tag Team Championship. The championship was founded by JWA in 1955, and has been active ever since (it moved to AJPW in 1976 following JWA's closure).
100. Madison Square Garden

Answers: Lethal Lottery

1. Two - The British Bulldog and William Regal

2. The staging area behind the entrance curtain.

3. True. He prevailed in a Pro Wrestling Iron six-man tag team match with Mike Modest & Donovan Morgan vs. Misawa, Yoshinari Ogawa, & Sal Thomaselli in 2004)

4. Chris Jericho

5. Anoa'i

6. They all the names of inanimate objects personified by wrestlers: Moppy (a mop, Perry Saturn), Mitch (a house plant, Dean Ambrose), Head (a mannequin's head, Al Snow), and Pepé (a hobby horse, Chavo Guerrero).

7. A 'worked' (fixed) outcome. The document appears to describe Demetrius accepting 3,800 drachmas to throw the match.

8. A babyface

9. El Torito (Ultimate Warrior: 89.9%; Hulk Hogan: 77.6%; Roddy Piper: 64.4%)

10. Power Slam

ANSWERS: LETHAL LOTTERY

11. *Marty Jannetty (one half of The Rockers with Shawn Michaels)*

12. *Jim Johnston*

13. *WWE Crush Hour*

14. *They all switched their attire to trunks.*

15. *The TitanTron*

16. *Dusty Rhodes and Mil Máscaras*

17. *Thesz was 21 years old when he won the American Wrestling Association World Heavyweight Championship in 1937.*

18. *Women*

19. *Seven (Randy Savage, Bret Hart, Steve Austin, Triple-H, Kurt Angle, Edge, Brock Lesnar. Ted DiBiase (1988's winner) illegitimately 'bought' the WWE World Heavyweight Championship from Andre the Giant; his reign is not recognised.*

20. *A time-limit draw*

21. *Bret Hart*

22. *Ric Flair*

23. *False (9-14)*

24. *Rikidozan vs. The Destroyer (Rikidozan vs. Lou Thesz on 6 October 1957 drew a larger television rating (87.0 compared to 67.0), but it had a lower overall viewing audience as fewer people owned television sets in Japan at the time.)*

25. *1999*

26. *They are all referees*

27. *South Park*

28. *Bill Apter*

29. *False. Arquette teamed with Alex Riley in a handicap match against Randy Orton on 13 December 2010.*

30. *6-11*

31. *Sky Low Low*

32. *Big Van Vader*

33. *True. Hogan was allegedly paid $30,000 to do the job.*

34. *WWE Confidential*

35. *Shotgun Saturday Night*

36. *Australia*

37. *Lance Storm*

38. *Bob Marella*

39. *902714*

40. *The SmackDown fist*

41. *Wayne Bloom*

42. *Layla. She won an NBA ring as part of Miami Heat's dance troupe in 2006.*

ANSWERS: LETHAL LOTTERY

43. *The Rock 'n' Roll Express and The Heavenly Bodies. The two teams faced one another at WCW SuperBrawl III in February, and on WWF Survivor Series '93 in November.*

44. *WrestleMania XIX (Kurt Angle vs. Brock Lesnar)*

45. *Korakuen Hall*

46. *Duane 'Gillberg' Gill*

47. *Randy Savage vs. Ric Flair (WrestleMania VIII and Starrcade '95)*

48. *Survivor Series '94 (Yokozuna vs. The Undertaker)*

49. *Miss Hancock*

50. *AJ Styles*

ND# THE ULTIMATE WRESTLING QUIZ BOOK

Photo Credits

The Territories
Page 12: Bruno Sammartino (Mike Lano)
Page 16: Mr Wrestling II (Mike Lano)
Page 18: Abdullah the Butcher (George Napolitano)
Page 19: Supertsar Billy Graham (George Napolitano)
Page 20: Fabulous Moolah (Ryan Brenna)
Page 21: Bruiser Brody (George Napolitano)
Page 22: Andre the Giant (George Napolitano)
Page 23: Pedro Morales (Ryan Brenna)
Page 25: Ric Flair (John Barrett)
Page 26: Hulk Hogan (John McFarlin)
Page 27: Iron Sheik (George Napolitano)

The Golden Era
Page 28: Hulk Hogan/Lou Albano/Cyndi Lauper (Adam Scull)
Page 30: David Schultz (George Napolitano)
Page 32: Dingo Warrior (Ryan Brenna)
Page 33: The Road Warriors (George Napolitano)
Page 33: Roddy Piper vs. Mr T (Adam Scull)
Page 34: Vince McMahon (Mike Lano)
Page 35: Dino Bravo (George Napolitano)
Page 36: Curt Hennig & Scott Hall (George Napolitano)
Page 37: Kevin Sullivan (George Napolitano)
Page 38: Hulk Hogan (George Napolitano)
Page 40: Randy Savage (George Napolitano)
Page 41: Sgt. Slaughter (George Napolitano)
Page 42: Beverly Brothers (George Napolitano)
Page 43: Miss Elizabeth (John Barrett)

A New Generation
Page 47: Glacier (George Tahinos)
Page 48: Sandman (George Tahinos)
Page 49: Diesel (John Barrett)
Page 50: Man Mountain Rock (George Tahinos)
Page 51: Hulk Hogan/Ric Flair (John Barrett)
Page 52: The Undertaker (John Barrett)
Page 53: Kama (John Barrett)
Page 54: Jean Pierre Lafitte (George Tahinos)
Page 54: Jeff Jarrett (John Barrett)
Page 55: Hakushi (George Tahinos)
Page 56: Duke Droese (George Tahinos)
Page 57: Brian Pillman (George Napolitano)
Page 58: Tekno Team 2000 (George Tahinos)
Page 61: Bret Hart (JF LeDuc)

Attitude
Page 64: Raven (George Tahinos)
Page 65: Cactus Jack (George Tahinos)
Page 66: Chae (George Tahinos)
Page 68: Goldberg (George Tahinos)
Page 69: Al Snow (George Napolitano)
Page 70: Butterbean (George Tahinos)
Page 74: Lita (Ryan Brenna)
Page 75: Meng (George Tahinos)
Page 77: Thunder Logo (George Tahinos)

PHOTO CREDITS

The Monopoly
Page 78: Triple H/Stephanie McMahon (John Barrett)
Page 80: Jeff Jarrett (Ryan Brenna)
Page 81: Triple H (Mike Lano)
Page 83: Mr America (John Barrett)
Page 84: Randy Orton (Matthew Balk)
Page 85: JBL (George Napolitano)
Page 86: Low Ki (George Tahinos)
Page 87: Jim Mitchell (George Tahinos)
Page 88: Umaga (George Napolitano)
Page 89: Steve Austin (George Napolitano)
Page 90: Matt Hardy (John Barrett)
Page 91: Brooke Hogan (JR Davis)
Page 92: Donald Trump/Vince McMahon/Bobby Lashley (George Napolitano)
Page 93: Shawn Michaels/Ric Flair (George Napolitano)
Page 95: John Cena/Shawn Michaels (George Napolitano)
The PG Era
Page 96: The Great Khali/Hornswoggle (George Napolitano)
Page 99: Kofi Kingston (Mike Mastrandrea)
Page 101: CM Punk (George Napolitano)
Page 103: Bryan Danielson (George Tahinos)
Page 106: Sin Cara (Bill Otton)
Page 107: Kharma (George Tahinos)
Page 108: Linda McMahon (John Barrett)
Page 109: AJ Lee (George Napolitano)
The Network
Page 112: The Wyatt Family (Ryan Brenna)
Page 114: Hideo Itami (Bill Otton)
Page 115: Rowan (Warren Keith)
Page 125: Cody (Scott Lesh)
Being Elite
Page 126: Chris Jericho (Scott Lesh)
Page 128: War Raiders (Tony Knox)
Page 129: Kairi Sane (Bill Otton)
Page 131: Teal Piper (Scott Lesh)
Page 132: The Kabuki Warriors (Ryan Brenna)
Page 133: Nightmare Collective (Scott Lesh)
Page 134: Cody/MJF (Scott Lesh)
Page 136: Kris Statlander (Scott Lesh)
Page 138: Sting (Scott Lesh)
Page 139: CM Punk (Scott Lesh)
Page 141: Kenny Omega (Scott Lesh)
Puroresu
Page 142: Antonio Inoki (George Napolitano)
Page 143: Giant Baba (George Napolitano)
Page 149: Ultimo Dragon (George Napolitano)
Page 157: Jushin Liger (Tony Knox)
Lethal Lottery
Page 158: Vader (George Napolitano)
Page 160: Triple H (John Barrett)
Page 161: Randy Savage (George Napolitano)
Page 163: Hulk Hogan/Jacques Rougeau (JF LeDuc)
All others images courtesy of the Inside the Ropes archive or public domain.